Year Around Conditioning
for
ARMY Football

This book is dedicated to Shar.

YEAR AROUND
CONDITIONING
FOR
ARMY FOOTBALL

- Strength Training
- Aerobic Endurance
- Flexibility
- Nutrition

Timothy Kearin

Leisure Press
P.O. Box 3
West Point, N.Y. 10996

A publication of Leisure Press.
P.O. Box 3, West Point, N.Y. 10996
Copyright © 1980 by Leisure Press
All rights reserved. Printed in the U.S.A.

ISBN 0-918438-60-8

Cover design by Tim and Sharon Kearin

Photographs in the Foreword used by permission of The U.S.M.A. Library. All action football photographs used by permission of U.S.M.A. Sports Information Office. All other photographs taken by Tim Kearin.

Appreciation is extended to the members of the Army football team for demonstrating the exercises in the photographs.

The views of the author do not purport to reflect the positions of the United States Military Academy, the Department of the Army, or the Department of Defense.

CONTENTS

Earl "Red" Blaik, Army Coach 1941-1958.

FOREWORD

Intercollegiate football began at West Point in 1890 as a result of a challenge from Navy who had been playing since 1882. In those days college football was characterized by mass plays depending on brute force. A newspaper report of the Yale vs Princeton game in 1885 said: "Came a crush about midway of the field. All the maddened giants of both teams were in it, and they lay heaped, choking, kicking, biting, gouging and howling. One smaller man lay under them. He held the ball hugged to his breast and pressed it to the ground." Prior to the first Army-Navy football game, West Point did not have a team. The only person at the academy who had ever played football before was Cadet Dennis Michie. It was through his organization and coaching that the first team developed. The first Army football uniforms consisted of white, laced, canvas jackets, white breeches, black woolen stockings and a black woolen cap.

The competitive edge of Navy's football experience was evident in that initial contest as Navy scored 12 points in each of the 45 minute halves and won 24-0. Following that loss Army realized that they needed expert coaching. The very next year, in November 1891, under the volunteer coaching efforts of Harry L. Williams, a former Yale football star, and Lieutenant Danny Tate, Army drove to their first victory over Navy by a score of 32-16.

Army-Navy Football at Annapolis, MD — November 28, 1891.

Army football continued to grow over the next 30 years. The most significant growth, however, occurred during Douglas MacArthur's tour of duty as Superintendent of USMA from 1919 through 1922. Under his direction Army began meeting major opponents other than Navy away from West Point. During his tenure as Superintendent, MacArthur delivered the famous words: "Upon the fields of friendly strife are sown the seeds that, upon other fields, on other days, will bear the fruits of victory." The seeds began to grow over the next 20 years until the formation of "Blaiks' Black Knights" materialized into the greatest team in the history of West Point. During 1944 and 1945 with Felix "Doc" Blanchard and Glenn Davis leading the rush, Army defeated teams such as: Pittsburgh 69-7, Notre Dame 59-0, Pennsylvania 62-7, Navy 32-13 and numerous other "big name" schools by a similarly large margin. West Point won National Football Championships from 1944-1946. Heisman Trophy "outstanding player in the nation" awards were given to "Doc" Blanchard 1945, Glenn Davis 1946, and Peter Dawkins 1958.

Heisman trophy winners Glen Davis (1946) and Felix "Doc" Blanchard (1945) with Coach Red Blaik.

Prior to the 1945 football era, teams with players weighing less than 200 pounds were commonplace. Little strength training was done up to that time because coaches believed that lifting weights resulted in tight muscles that restricted range and speed of movement (muscle bound). After World War II, Dr. T.L. De Lorme began pioneering work in the area of weight training for rehabilitation purposes. Strength training was used to restore strength to various areas of the body on injured military veterans. Acceptance of weight training by the medical field stimulated researchers in the physical education profession to put the "muscle bound" myth to rest. Since that time, almost all major college football powers have trained with weights.

West Point has had several successful seasons since "Blaiks' Black Knights" but has not been able to achieve the consistency that other successful football teams have had. Although there may be several reasons for this, one apparent factor is the lack of size and strength that many major teams have as a result of "year around training." Although Army has utilized strength training in recent years, it has only been an off-season goal. In order to rectify the limitations inherent in a conditioning program which involves only part of the calendar year, a concerted effort to keep Army a top competitor in major college football has resulted in—*"Year Around Conditioning For Army Football."*

A stronger athlete is a better athlete.

1 BASIC PRINCIPLES OF STRENGTH TRAINING

Muscle Structure

The human body has nearly 450 muscles which are responsible for man's movement and basic function. The muscles involved in the movement of the body are called skeletal muscles. These are the muscles that permit the function of skill. The major muscles are shown in Figure 1-1. Skeletal muscles consist of long cylindrical bunches of muscle fibers. Each bundle of fibers is bound together by a sheath of connective tissue. The ends of the connective tissue form tendons which attach the whole muscle to the bone. Within each muscle bundle are numerous muscle fibers that vary in dimension from microscopic size to the thickness of a fine human hair. Each individual fiber contains a muscle cell, numerous column shaped structures called myofibrils and protein material known as mitochondria.

Muscular contraction occurs when the motor unit receives a transmission from the central nervous system. A motor unit is made up of the nerve cell and its branching nerve fibers and is also known as a neuromuscular unit. One nerve cell may innervate several muscle fibers or as few as one. The ratio of nerve fibers to muscle fibers varies depending on the degree of precision that is required of the muscle. The total number of muscle fibers that can be recruited for a single muscular contraction is defined as neuromuscular efficiency, a factor which has important implications for the potential of muscular strength.

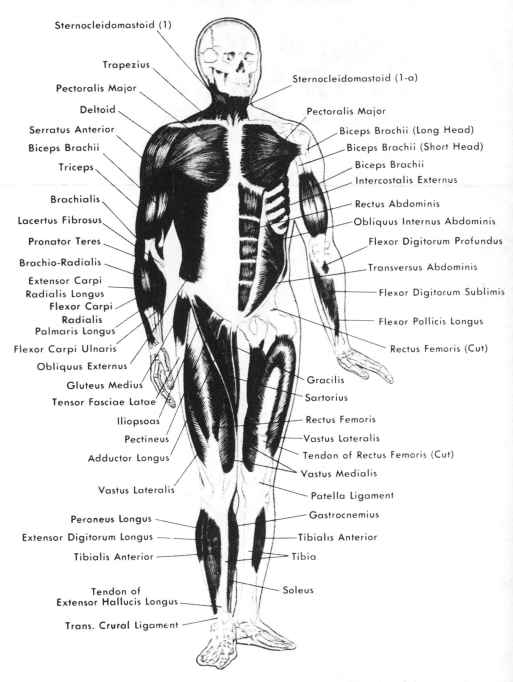

Figure 1-1(a). Muscles of the body: anterior view. (Reprinted by permission of Cramer Products Inc.)

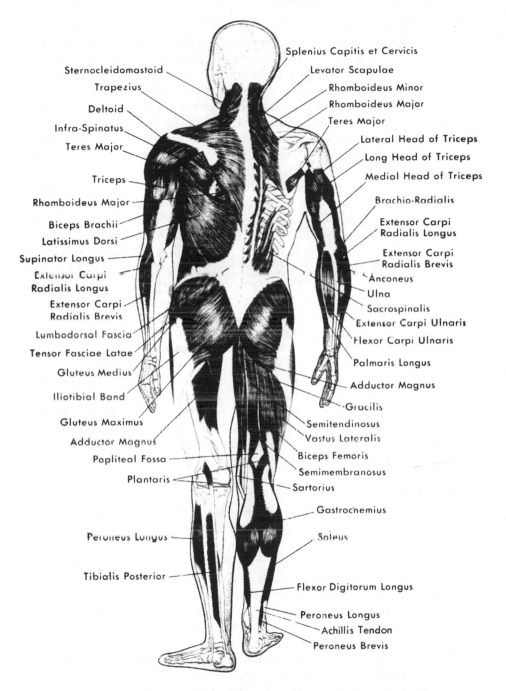

Figure 1-1(b). Muscles of the body: posterior view. (Reprinted by permission of Cramer Products Inc.)

Physiology of Strength

Muscle tissue is very specific in that the muscle only provides as much strength as necessary to perform normal daily tasks. When the demand becomes greater than the muscle is normally accustomed to, the strength and size of the muscle increases. This phenomenon is known as hypertrophy. The number of fibers within a muscle is genetically determined. To date, research has shown that this number is not affected by training. Research has proven however, that the number of myofibrils and the size and number of mitochondria within the muscle fiber, in fact, increase as the result of training. A properly conducted weight training program exceeds an individual's normal requirement for muscular function and becomes the overload principle that results in hypertrophy. As the muscle adapts to the new requirement the overload principle must again be applied in order to stimulate a new strength change. This is known as progressive resistance exercise. As long as a muscle has reserve strength (has not been exercised to fatigue) i.e. an exercise is terminated at 9 repetitions when it could have continued until 12 or more, the stimulus for hypertrophy is not present. Therefore, in order to stimulate a strength increase it is necessary to continue the exercise to the point where it is momentarily impossible to perform another repetition in good form.

On the other hand, when a muscle is not stressed to a point at least as high as it is normally accustomed to, the muscle will shrink in size (atrophy). An excellent example of what occurs with atrophy can be observed when a limb is removed from a cast after it has been immobilized for a few weeks. The muscles shrink considerably because the stimulus for strength has not been present.

The proper method of applying the overload principle will be discussed in detail later in this chapter.

Warm-Up

A great deal of controversy exists concerning the benefits associated with a warming-up period prior to a weight training workout. It has traditionally been accepted that a warm-up program, since it raises muscle and blood temperature, can significantly improve any athletic performance. Warming up seems to make its largest contribution in activities involving muscular strength and power. The greatest benefit seems to be its importance in preventing muscle pulls and tears. This will be discussed in greater detail in the chapter on flexibility.

Every weight workout should always be preceded by a 10 minute warming-up period. The exact amount of time necessary may vary with each individual but should at a minimum include the following: Slow jogging or running in place, light calisthenics such as jumping jacks and slow static stretching. Additionally, each maximal or near maximal lift attempt should always be preceded by lifting a lighter weight through the full range of movement for 8 to 10 repetitions.

Regardless of the activity, and particularly while performing strength training exercises, warming-up is always a good practice to follow.

Muscle Soreness

It is very common for localized soreness to occur when an exercise program involves overexertion of a muscle. Soreness usually appears during a 24 to 48 hour period following the exercise. The exact cause of muscle soreness is subject to controversy. One common theory hypothesizes that overexertion causes an accumulation of lactic acid (the end product of energy production) creating pressure against the tissue. The most recent theory suggests that the negative (lowering) portion of the exercise causes a strain of the connective tissue. Regardless of the cause, the result can be considerable discomfort.

Totally preventing muscle soreness is almost impossible in a well-designed progressive weight training program. The following practices, however, can help prevent or minimize severe muscle soreness: (1) a proper warm-up including static stretching; (2) a very slow increase in workload; (3) attempting to avoid jerky, bouncing type movements of the resistance. Once muscle soreness does occur the best relief will come from static stretching and continued exercise.

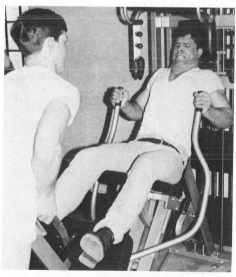

To stimulate a maximum strength increase, it is necessary to perform an exercise to the point where it is momentarily impossible to perform another repetition in good form.

Range of Movement

The range of motion in a skeletal joint is affected largely by the musculature surrounding the joint. Since muscle tissue has elasticity and extensibility, training with a limited joint motion during a strength exercise will cause the muscle to lose elasticity and shorten. Continued training in this manner will result in a loss of flexibility. To an athlete this means decreasing functional ability and increasing the chances of injury.

Many types of equipment on the market today are designed to isolate muscle groups and provide an even resistance through the full range of movement. Equipment, such as barbells, limit the range of movement in certain exercises. An example is the bench press. This exercise limits the range of movement for the shoulder joints when the bar touches the chest (Fig. 1-2). When the bench press is performed with the barbell it should always be accompanied by the parallel bar dip (Fig. 1-3). The same muscles are involved in this movement and the exercise permits maximal range of movement.

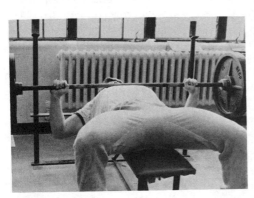

Figure 1-2.   **Figure 1-3.**

The Universal Gym has a bench press station that allows for a greater range of movement by having the bar curve around the chest. As noted in the example (Fig. 1-4) however, the range of movement frequently becomes limited because the weight stack hits the bottom before the bar reaches the chest of the average person. The range of movement on this apparatus can be increased simply by placing a block of wood under the bench (Fig. 1-5). Note that the bar now permits maximum range of movement.

Regardless of the type of equipment used, every exercise should allow movement of the resistance through the greatest range the joint will permit. When an athlete exercises properly, the flexibility of his joints will actually *increase*.

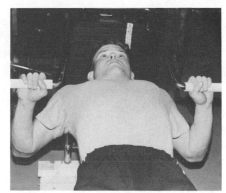

Figure 1-4.   **Figure 1-5.**

Repetitions

A repetition is defined as the movement of a resistance through the full range of motion. For weight training purposes the movement is divided into two parts: The positive portion and the negative portion. The positive por tion occurs when the muscle shortens as the resistance is raised. This phase is referred to scientifically as a "concentric contraction." As the resistance is lowered and the muscle lengthens, the negative portion occurs. This phase is labeled the "eccentric contraction." For the remainder of this book, the movement during a repetition will be referred to as positive or negative.

It is important to understand both parts of the repetition because the negative portion is frequently misunderstood. In the two arm curl (Fig. 1-6), it is incorrect to believe that the biceps raise the weight and the triceps lower the weight. The fact is that the biceps raise the weight with a positive con- traction and the same muscles (biceps) lower the weight with a negative contraction.

A properly performed repetition should take approximately six seconds. The positive portion should take two seconds and the negative twice as long or four seconds. A negative contraction produces about fifty percent more strength and will benefit more at the slower rate. When the first repetition is completed, the next repetition should begin without pausing at the starting position. The repetitions in an exercise should continue until momentary muscular failure occurs. This is the point where it becomes momentarily im- possible to move the resistance any further in good form. For maximal results, the point of momentary failure should occur at a point between 8 and 12 repetitions. Recent research indicates that the leg muscles may benefit more by reaching momentary failure between 12 and 15 repetitions. The method for increasing the resistance will be discussed later in this chapter.

Bicep

Figure 1-6. *The bicep raises the weight with a positive contraction and lowers the weight with a negative contraction.*

Proper Breathing

A proper method of breathing is extremely important while performing weight training exercises. It is a common practice to hold the breath while performing an exercise such as the bench press, because a stabilized rib cage provides more support for the working muscles of the chest. Such a practice, however, can cause dizziness, headaches and even loss of consciousness in extreme cases. This occurance is called the Valsalva maneuver. As the exercise is performed the air in the lungs (which is held in by a closed windpipe) exerts pressure against the heart. This results in reduced cardiac output inhibiting the ability of the heart to pump oxygenated blood to the working muscles and the brain.

The most efficient method of breathing is to exhale while doing the positive (lifting) portion of the repetition and to inhale while doing the negative (lowering) portion of the repetition. An exchange of breath should occur during each repetition. Proper breathing also plays an important role in the production of energy when numerous repetitions are performed.

Sets

A set is equal to the total number of repetitions performed in an exercise. The correct number of sets of each exercise varies with the type of equipment used. For best results a muscle should be exhausted through the full range of movement in as few sets as possible. Additional sets interfere with the muscle's ability to recover entirely by the next workout.

An appropriate number of sets when exercising with barbells is three. A barbell provides resistance in a straight line and limits the weakest part of the movement. Since there is minimal leverage at the beginning of the movement, it is at this point when momentary muscular failure occurs. The muscle is only partially exhausted when the first set is completed. Two additional sets performed in the same manner will cause maximal exhaustion. The first set should reach the point of failure between 8 and 10 repetitions with the resistance remaining the same for the next two sets when a total of three sets are performed. When 12 or more repetitions can be completed in the first set and at least 10 repetitions in the third, the resistance should be increased by an additional 5 to 10 percent.

Nautilus equipment provides accommodating resistance. Each machine has a cam (Fig. 1-7) that varies the resistance to accommodate the leverage advantages and disadvantages throughout the full range of the specific muscle exercised. When using this type of apparatus the entire muscle is exhausted in one set. As with the barbells the resistance should be increased by 5 to 10 percent when more than 12 repetitions can be performed.

Figure 1-7. The "cam" varies the resistance to accommodate the full range of a muscle's strength curve.

Recovery Time

There are two recovery periods that effect maximal gains in weight training. The first recovery period is the amount of time between each exercise and the second period is the amount of time between each workout. When the exercises are done with barbells the second and third set should begin as soon as the muscles have recovered enough to exert another maximal effort. The interval should not exceed two or three minutes at a maximum. If a maximal effort cannot be exerted, i.e. the first set ends at 11 repetitions and the next set at 6 repetitions, the rest period was too brief. The interval between exercises involving different muscles can be as fast as the individual can move to the next piece of equipment. When using equipment such as Nautilus and training with minimal rest between each different exercise, an individual's level of cardiorespiratory fitness can be improved as well.

The second recovery period concerns the time interval between complete work-outs. If a muscle is exercised to the point of exhaustion it needs at least 48 hours to recover. If the same muscle was exercised everyday, then the muscle's ability to recover and meet the new demand would be exceeded and the muscle would actually become weaker. On the other hand, if that same muscle was not maximally stimulated again within 72 hours of the previous workout the muscle would begin to atrophy or shrink in size. It is for this reason that exercises for the same muscle are done every other day or three times per week allowing for a two day rest on the weekends.

Split Routines

A complete body workout with barbells may take as long as an hour and a half. If only forty-five minutes are available for a daily workout the individual may elect to split the workout. This can be done in two ways: *Upper body* on Monday, Wednesday and Friday, and *lower body* on Tuesday, Thursday and Saturday; or *pushing exercises* i.e. bench press, seated press, tricep extensions and squats on Monday, Wednesday and Friday, and *pulling exercises* i.e. bentover rowing, lat. pulldowns, bicep curls and leg curls on Tuesday, Thursday and Saturday.

Split routines can be accomplished successfully because each individual muscle group is given a 48 hour recovery period. Ideally, a whole body workout should be accomplished in one time frame with the next day allowing the muscular system to rest. Aerobic work such as jogging can be done daily along with weight workouts, or every other day on the off weight day. Jogging is a sub-maximal workout and does not require the same total recovery as a weight workout.

Order of Exercises

During each workout a specific order of exercises should be followed. For best results the largest muscles should always be exercised first. The correct order of exercises are as follows: buttocks (gluteus maximus), thighs (quadriceps), calves (gastrocnemius), foot flexors (tibialis anterior), chest (pectoralis major), back (latissimus dorsi), shoulders (deltoids), upper arms (biceps/triceps), lower arms (wrist flexors/extensors), stomach (abdominals) and neck (flexor/extensor group). The major reason for this progression is to insure that a supporting muscle is not too exhausted to support the trunk while a major muscle group is being exercised. For example, if the stomach muscles were exhausted prior to performing a full squat, the individual could collapse because the supporting muscles of the trunk were too fatigued to provide stability for the trunk.

The progression of exercises as listed above is not always possible. If there is a large number of individuals ready to workout and a limited amount of equipment, the workout for the entire body could be separated into two major areas: the upper body and the lower body. Once a weight training program is started, an attempt should be made to always repeat the same order so that the athlete's progress can be charted accurately.

For best results, the largest muscles should always be exercised first.

Workout Cards

All workout information with the exception of warm-ups should be recorded. It is very difficult to recall the exact weight and number of repetitions performed in the previous workout without a progress chart. An example of a workout card is shown at Figure 1-8. The example displays a card that is used for upper body exercises with barbells. The other side of the card is used for lower body and any additional exercises. Workout information should be recorded immediately after each exercise is completed (Fig. 1-9). The top of the card can be used to record date and body weight.

A workout card for variable resistance equipment is designed in a different manner (Fig. 1-10). Since only one set of each exercise is performed, only one line per exercise is used. It should be noted that a letter designation rather than a number is recorded. Letters are placed on the weight stack so that the lifter is not as concerned with the amount of weight that is being lifted. The emphasis here is on quality rather than quantity.

Name _____

Phone _____

FREE WEIGHTS WORKOUT

BODY WEIGHT										
UPPER BODY										
Rowing										
Press										
Pullover										
Side Raise										
OTHER — Curls										
French Curls										
Shrugs										

Figure 1-8.

BENCH PRESS

DATE	1-1	1-3	1-5	1-8	1-10	1-12	1-15
BODY WEIGHT	180	181	179	182	182	182	184
1	100/11	100/12	100/13	105/10	105/12	105/13	110/9
2	100/9	100/10	100/11	105/9	105/10	105/11	110/8
3	100/8	100/8	100/10	105/8	105/9	105/10	110/8

LEG EXTENSION	G/11	G/12	G/14	G/16	H/10	H/12	H/11	H/13
LEG PRESS	K/18	L/13	M/14	M/14	M/15	M/16	N/12	N/12
LEG CURL	E/6	C/16	D/12	D/13	D/15	D/15	E/10	E/12

Figure 1-9. *The resistance should be increased when more than 12 repetitions can be performed on the first set and at least 10 repetitions on the third set.*

Figure 1-10. *Only one set of repetitions in each exercise is performed on variable resistance equipment.*

24

Negative Training

The negative (lowering) portion of each repetition in an exercise is just as important as the positive portion for building strength. Some researchers believe that the negative portion is even more important. From a flexibility standpoint, it is the negative part of the exercise that stretches the muscle tissue and allows for a more flexible joint. The strength potential in lowering the resistance is considerably greater than raising the resistance. When the point of momentary failure is reached in an exercise only the positive (lifting) capability of the muscle has been fully exhausted. Since the muscle's ability to lower the resistance continues, a further state of muscular exhaustion can be reached.

There are two popular methods of practicing negative training in a weight program. The first method is performed with a partner and may be done in one of the two ways: (1) The lifter exercises to the point of momentary failure e.g. 9½ repetitions and then the partner assists in the positive movement (Fig. 1-11) and the lifter performs the negative movement unassisted. (2) The partner assists with the positive movement (after momentary failure has been reached) and applies additional resistance (Fig. 1-12) with the hands placed on the weight stack or against the counter balance. The negative repetitions should continue until the lifter can no longer control the lowering movement unassisted. This negative work should not exceed an additional four repetitions.

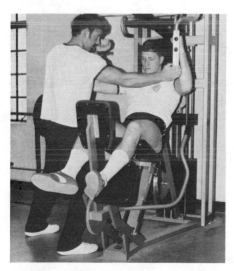

Figure 1-11.

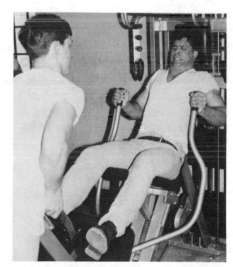

Figure 1-12.

The second method is called negative accentuated exercise and can be performed without the assistance of a partner. This exercise can only be performed on equipment such as Nautilus (Fig. 1-13) or Universal Gym (Fig. 1-14) where the weight stack is connected to the lifting apparatus for both limbs. The positive portion of each repetition is performed with two limbs and the negative portion is performed with one limb. During the next repetition the weight is lowered with the other limb and the exercise continues in an alternate manner until the positive portion can no longer be continued.

Negative exercise adds an additional overload and can provide rapid strength increases if it is done properly. A practical approach is to perform negative work at the completion of each exercise. This type of training should not exceed two workouts per week. If strength progress begins to decline and everything else is being performed properly then the amount of negative work may be exceeding the recovery capability of the muscle. When this occurs, the amount of negative work should be reduced.

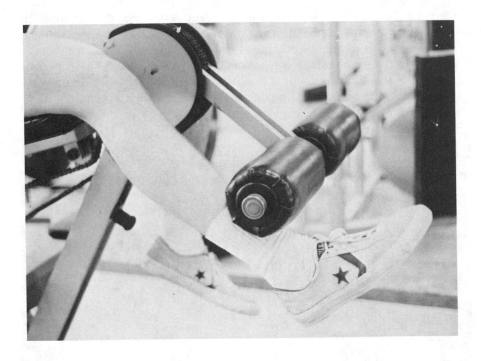

Figure 1-13. *This is an example of negative accentuated exercise on the leg extension machine.*

Figure 1-14. *The positive part of the move-ment is performed with two limbs and the negative part with one limb.*

Safety

A strength training program is a very safe activity as long as the basic principles of weight training are adhered to. However, before a program is initiated a few basic considerations should be made.

a. If in poor medical condition, consult a medical doctor.
b. If recovering from a joint injury, wait until an unrestricted range of movement has returned.
c. Always use spotters for exercises when the negative movement is performed first, i.e. the bench press with barbells or the full squat.
d. Always wear shoes with rubber soles.
e. Use collars on barbells.
f. Do not drop weights.
g. Avoid jerky or bouncing movements.
h. Use common sense.

The primary advantage of free weights are that they are relatively inexpensive, they can be found at almost any school which has a gymnasium, and they require the athlete to maintain control and balance throughout the exercise.

2 FREE WEIGHT EXERCISES

The purpose of this chapter is to describe exercises that can be performed with any type of "free weight" apparatus. This equipment includes barbells, dumbbells, or any other device that allows movement through a range of motion, yet is unattached to a stabilized apparatus. The advantages of "free weights" are that they are inexpensive, they can be found at almost any school that has a gymnasium, and they require the athlete to maintain control and balance throughout the exercise.

This chapter contains descriptions and illustrations of strength training exercises using "free weight" equipment. These exercises should be performed using the techniques described in Chapter 1. Also included is a sample "free weight" workout. The correct order in which to perform these exercises is as follows:

1. Dead Lift	12. Bent Over Flys
2. Parallel Squat	13. Seated Press Behind Neck
3. Leg Curl	14. Side Lateral Raise
4. Leg Extension	15. Upright Row
5. Heel Raise	16. Shoulder Shrug
6. Foot Flexion	17. Bicep Curl
7. Bench Press	18. French Curl
8. Bent Arm Flys	19. Wrist Curls
9. Parallel Dips	20. Reverse Wrist Curl
10. Chin-Ups	21. Sit-Ups
11. Bent Over Rowing	22. 4-Way Neck with Partner

Dead Lift

Equipment Used: Barbell
Major Muscles Involved: Spinal erectors, gluteus maximus, quadriceps
Description of Exercise:
1. Stand with feet slightly greater than shoulder width.
2. Squat and grip bar with an underhand grip on non-dominant hand and an overhand grip on dominant hand.
3. Keep elbows outside of knees and head up.
4. Pull bar straightening legs and back until standing straight with shoulders back.
5. Pause, slowly recover to starting position and repeat.
Important Points:
1. Keep back straight and lift with legs.
2. Keep bar close to shins throughout the exercise.
3. Roll shoulders back at completion of positive movement.

Dead Lift: Starting Position

Dead Lift: Pause Position

Parallel Squat

Equipment Used: Barbell
Major Muscles Involved: Gluteus maximus, quadriceps
Description of Exercise:
1. Place barbell on back of shoulders and assume a comfortable grip.
2. Spread feet slightly greater than shoulder width and point toes slightly outward.
3. Squat slowly downward in a knee bend until tops of thighs are parallel with floor.
4. Pause, recover to starting position and repeat.

Important Points:
1. Keep head up and back straight throughout the movement.
2. Do not bounce at bottom of movement.
3. Heel supports such as 2½ lb. plates may be used until ankle flexibility increases.
4. Since this exercise begins with the negative movement always use spotters.

Parallel Squat: Starting Position

Parallel Squat: Pause Position

31

Leg Curl

Equipment Used: No equipment necessary
Major Muscles Involved: Hamstrings
Description of Exercise:

1. Lay flat on ground with both legs extended.
2. Partner places hands behind left heel.
3. While partner applies resistance curl foot as high as possible (at least perpendicular).
4. Pause, slowly recover to starting position and repeat.
5. When left leg is exhausted perform same exercise with right leg.

Important Points:

1. Partner should apply enough resistance so that a maximum effort takes two seconds for the positive movement and four seconds for the negative.
2. Keep body flat on ground.

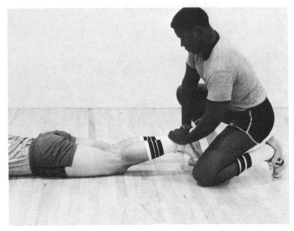

Leg Curl: Starting Position

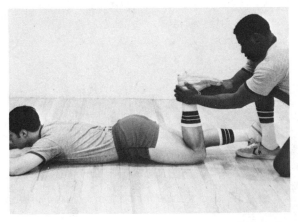

Leg Curl: Pause Position

Leg Extension

Equipment Used: No equipment necessary
Major Muscles Involved: Quadriceps
Description of Exercise:
1. Lay flat on ground with left leg flexed as far as possible.
2. Partner places hands in front of left foot.
3. While partner applies resistance push foot back and downward until leg is extended.
4. Pause, slowly recover to starting position and repeat.
5. When left leg is exhausted perform same exercise with right leg.
Important Points:
1. Partner should apply enough resistance so that a maximum effort takes two seconds for the positive movement and four seconds for the negative.
2. Do not raise knee off of ground.

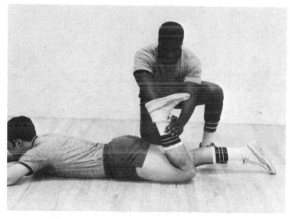

Leg Extension: Starting Position

Leg Extension: Pause Position

Heel Raise

Equipment Used: Barbell
Major Muscles Involved: Calves
Description of Exercise:
1. Place barbell across shoulders and assume a comfortable grip with hands.
2. Spread feet shoulder width apart and place balls of feet on block of wood.
3. Elevate heels as high as possible.
4. Pause, slowly recover to starting position and repeat.
Important Points:
1. Keep back straight and head up.
2. Do not rest when heels touch ground.

Heel Raise: Starting Position   *Heel Raise: Pause Position*

Foot Flexion

Equipment Used: Towel
Major Muscles Involved: Tibialis anterior
Description of Exercise:
1. Sit on ground with both legs extended and feet flexed.
2. Partner loops towel over toes on right foot.
3. Partner applies enough resistance so that a maximum effort takes two seconds for the positive movement and four seconds for the negative.
4. Pause, slowly recover to starting position and repeat.
5. When right leg is exhausted repeat exercise with left leg.
Important Points:
1. Place towel high on toes for maximum leverage.
2. Keep knee straight throughout movement.

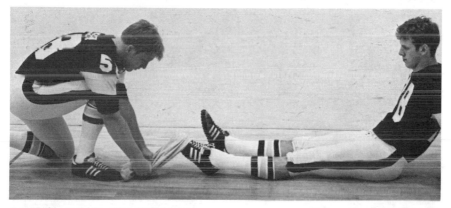

Foot Flexion: Starting Position

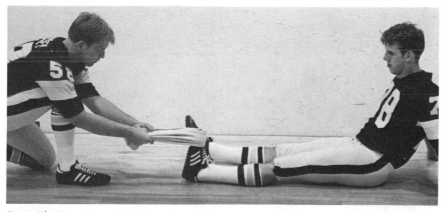

Foot Flexion: Pause Position

Bench Press

Equipment Used: Barbell
Major Muscles Involved: Pectorals, deltoids, triceps
Description of Exercise:
1. Lay flat on bench with back of shoulders and buttocks flat on bench.
2. Bend knees and place feet flat on floor.
3. Grip bar slightly wider than shoulder width.
4. Lower bar to center of chest and pause.
5. Push arms upward until elbows are extended and repeat.

Important Points:
1. Do not raise buttocks off of bench.
2. Do not bounce weight off of chest.
3. Exhale while raising the weight.
4. When using near maximum weight utilize spotters.

Bench Press: Starting Position

Bench Press: Pause Position

Bent Arm Flys

Equipment Used: Dumbbells
Major Muscles Involved: Pectorals, deltoids
Description of Exercise:
1. Lay flat on bench with knees bent and feet flat on floor.
2. Hold dumbbells over chest with elbows slightly bent, palms facing inward and dumbbells touching each other.
3. Slowly lower dumbbells outward and downward keeping elbows bent until maximum stretch is reached.
4. Pause, recover to starting position and repeat.

Important Points:
1. Keep elbows slightly bent throughout exercise.
2. Raise and lower arms as if hugging a barrel.

Bent Arm Flys: Starting Position

Bent Arms Flys: Pause Position

Parallel Dips

Equipment Used: Parallel Bars
Major Muscles Involved: Pectorals, deltoids, triceps
Description of Exercise:
1. Grip parallel bars with palms facing inward.
2. Suspend weight with elbows slightly bent and knees bent.
3. Slowly lower body bending elbows as far as possible.
4. Pause, recover to starting position and repeat.
Important Points:
1. Do not swing body during exercise.
2. Pause at bottom of movement.

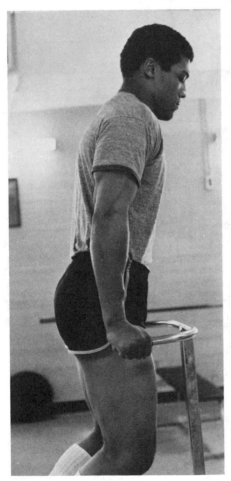

Parallel Dips: Starting Position   *Parallel Dips: Pause Position*

Chin-Ups

Equipment Used: Any sturdy bar
Major Muscles Involved: Latissimus dorsi, biceps
Description of Exercise:
1. Grip bar with an underhand grip and hands shoulder width apart.
2. Hang from bar with elbows straight.
3. Raise body upward until chin is above bar.
4. Pause, slowly recover to starting position and repeat.
Important Points:
1. Do not allow body to swing during exercise.
2. Allow elbows to extend completely at bottom of movement.

Chin-Ups: Starting Position   *Chin-Ups: Pause Position*

Bent Over Rowing

Equipment Used: Barbell
Major Muscles Involved: Latissimus dorsi, biceps
Description of Exercise:
1. Stand with feet shoulder width apart and knees slightly bent.
2. Bend forward at waist until torso is parallel with floor.
3. Grip bar with an overhand grip and hands greater than shoulder width apart.
4. Raise bar to center of chest.
5. Pause, slowly lower resistance to starting position and repeat.
Important Points:
1. Keep head up and back straight.
2. Keep back parallel with floor.

Bent Over Rowing: Starting Position

Bent Over Rowing: Pause Position

Bent Over Flys

Equipment Used: Dumbbells
Major Muscles Involved: Latissimus dorsi, rhomboids
Description of Exercise:
1. Stand with feet shoulder width apart and knees slightly bent.
2. Bend forward at waist until torso is parallel with floor.
3. Grip dumbbells with palms facing inward, arms straight, and dumbbells touching each other.
4. Raise arms laterally as high as possible.
5. Pause, slowly recover to starting position and repeat.
Important Points:
1. Keep head up and back straight.
2. Keep back parallel to floor throughout exercise.

Bent Over Fly: Starting Position

Bent Over Fly: Pause Position

Seated Press Behind Neck

Equipment Used: Barbell
Major Muscles Involved: Deltoids, triceps
Description of Exercise:
1. Sit on bench with feet flat on floor.
2. Grip barbell greater than shoulder width and place on back of shoulders.
3. Extend arms overhead until elbows are straight.
4. Pause, slowly recover to starting position and repeat.
Important Points:
1. Lower bar slowly and do not bounce off of neck.
2. Do not arch back as it places stress on the lower back.

*Press Behind Neck:
Starting Position*

*Press Behind Neck:
Pause Position*

Side Lateral Raise

Equipment Used: Dumbbells
Major Muscles Involved: Deltoids
Description of Exercise:
1. Stand with feet shoulder width apart and arms extended downward.
2. Face palms inward holding dumbbells at side.
3. Raise dumbbells laterally until arms are parallel with floor.
4. Pause, slowly recover to starting position.
Important Points:
1. Stand as straight as possible.
2. Do not raise weights above shoulder level as other muscles will become involved.

Lateral Raise: Starting Position

Lateral Raise: Pause Position

Upright Row

Equipment Used: Barbell
Major Muscles Involved: Deltoids, trapezius
Description of Exercise:
1. Stand with feet shoulder width apart and arms extended downward.
2. Grip bar with an overhand grip narrower than shoulder width.
3. Pull bar upward without bending torso until bar touches chin.
4. Pause, slowly recover to starting position and repeat.
Important Points:
1. Stand straight with head up throughout exercise.
2. Pull bar all the way to chin.

Upright Row: Starting Position

Upright Row: Pause Position

Shoulder Shrug

Equipment Used: Barbell
Major Muscles Involved: Trapezius
Description of Exercise:
1. Stand with feet shoulder width apart and arms extended downward.
2. Grip bar with an overhand grip, hands shoulder width apart.
3. Keep arms straight and raise shoulders as high as possible.
4. Pause, slowly recover to starting position and repeat.
Important Points:
1. Stand straight throughout exercise.
2. Allow shoulders to drop as far as possible at bottom of movement.

Shoulder Shrug: Starting Position

Shoulder Shrug: Pause Position

Bicep Curl

Equipment Used: Barbell or easy curl bar
Major Muscles Involved: Biceps
Description of Exercise:
1. Stand with feet less than shoulder width and arms extended downward.
2. Grip bar with an underhand grip, hands just outside of hips.
3. Keep elbows back and curl bar as high as possible.
4. Pause, slowly recover to starting position and repeat.
Important Points:
1. Keep back straight and do not lean back.
2. Keep elbows back throughout exercise.

Bicep Curl: Starting Position   *Bicep Curl: Pause Position*

French Curl

Equipment Used: Barbell
Major Muscles Involved: Triceps
Description of Exercise:
1. Lay flat on bench with knees bent and feet flat on floor.
2. Grip bar with an overhand grip and hands narrower than shoulder width.
3. Upper arms should be perpendicular to floor with bar just above forehead.
4. Extend arms upward until elbows are straight.
5. Pause, slowly recover to starting position and repeat.

Important Points:
1. Keep upper arms perpendicular throughout exercise.
2. Keep elbows at shoulder width throughout exercise.

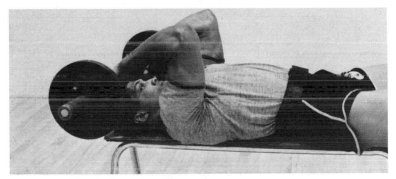

French Curl: Starting Position

French Curl: Pause Position

Wrist Curl

Equipment Used: Barbell
Major Muscles Involved: Forearm flexors
Description of Exercise:
1. Sit on end of bench with knees bent and feet flat on floor.
2. Place forearms firmly against thighs.
3. Grip bar with an underhand grip and allow bar to roll to finger tips.
4. Curl fingers upward and flex wrists.
5. Pause, slowly recover to starting position and repeat.
Important Points:
1. Keep forearms in contact with thighs throughout exercise.
2. Allow fingers to extend downward as far as possible at bottom of movement.

Wrist Curl: Starting Position

Wrist Curl: Pause Position

Reverse Wrist Curl

Equipment Used: Barbell
Major Muscles Involved: Forearm extensors
Description of Exercise:
1. Sit on end of bench with knees bent and feet flat on floor.
2. Place forearms firmly against thighs.
3. Grip bar with overhand grip and allow wrists to bend downward.
4. Curl wrists upward and backward as far as possible.
5. Pause, slowly recover to starting position and repeat.
Important Points:
1. Keep forearms in contact with thighs throughout the exercise.
2. Keep wrists just over ends of knees.

Reverse Wrist Curl:
Starting Position

Reverse Wrist Curl:
Pause Position

Sit-Up

Equipment Used: Cushions
Major Muscles Involved: Abdominals
Description of Exercise:
1. Sit on floor with cushions placed under buttocks.
2. Bend knees and place feet flat on floor.
3. Partner holds feet in place.
4. Lace fingers behind head and lay torso one inch from floor.
5. Curl torso upward to a point just short of vertical.
6. Pause, slowly recover to starting position and repeat.

Important Points:
1. Pause torso just short of vertical or abdominals will be allowed to relax.
2. When more than 15 repetitions can be performed, place a 10 pound plate behind head.

Sit-Up: Starting Position

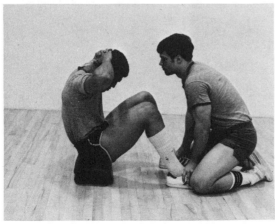

Sit-Up: Pause Position

Neck Exercises: Anterior Flexion

Equipment Used: No equipment necessary
Major Muscles Involved: Anterior flexors
Description of Exercise:
1. Assume a kneeling position on all fours and raise head as high as possible.
2. Partner places hands on front of forehead.
3. While partner provides resistance push head down towards chest.
4. Pause, slowly recover to starting position and repeat.
Important Points:
1. Move head smoothly throughout movement.
2. Partner should interlace fingers and cradle forehead in hands.

Anterior Flexion: Starting Position

Anterior Flexion: Pause Position

Posterior Extension: Starting Position

Posterior Extension: Pause Position

Neck Exercises: Posterior Extension

Equipment Used: No equipment necessary
Major Muscles Involved: Posterior extensors
Description of Exercise:
1. Assume a kneeling position on all fours.
2. Lower head to chest.
3. Partner places hands on back of head.
4. While partner applies resistance raise head as high as possible.
5. Pause, slowly recover to starting position and repeat.
Important Points:
1. Partner should stand where he can apply smooth resistance.
2. Partners must communicate.

Neck Exercises: Lateral Flexion-Left and Right

Equipment Used: No equipment necessary
Major Muscles Involved: Lateral Flexors
Description of Exercise:

1. Assume a kneeling position on all fours.
2. Turn head as far as possible towards left shoulder.
3. Partner places hands and knee against right ear.
4. While partner applies resistance push head as far as possible toward right shoulder.
5. Pause, slowly recover to starting position and repeat.

Important Points:

1. Enough resistance should be applied so that it takes two seconds for the positive and four seconds for the negative.
2. Partners should practice this exercise.

Lateral Flexion: Starting Position

Lateral Flexion: Pause Position

Sample Free Weight Workout

Monday and Friday

Exercise	Number of Sets
Dead Lift	3
Squat	3
Leg Curl with Partner	1
Leg Extension with Partner	1
Heel Raise	3
Foot Flexion with Partner	1
Bench Press	3
Bent Arm Flys	2
Chin Ups	2
Bent Over Flys	2
Seated Press	3
Side Lateral Raise	2
Shoulder Shrugs	2
Bicep Curls	3
Tricep Extension	3
Wrist Curls	1
Reverse Wrist Curls	1
Sit-Ups	1
4 Way Neck with Partner	1

Wednesday

Squat	3
Leg Curl with Partner	1
Bench Press	2
Bent Over Row	2
Seated Press	2
Parallel Dips	2
Shoulder Shrugs	1
Bicep Curls	2
Tricep Extensions	2
Sit-Ups	1

Adherence to scientifically-based strength training principles is an absolute must if an athlete is to maximize his strength gains.

3 UNIVERSAL GYM EXERCISES

A Universal Gym (or any other multi-station apparatus, e.g. Paramount, Pro-Gym, etc.) can be found in nearly every major college, most high schools, and numerous Y.M.C.A.'s throughout the country. These machines are popular because they are easy to use, do not require spotters, have built in safety features, handle fairly large groups at the same time, and are relatively inexpensive.

The program included in this chapter is designed to be performed using the principles stated in Chapter 1. All of the major exercises which can be performed on nearly every Universal are described in this chapter. Also included is a sample Universal Gym workout.

For best results the exercises should be performed in this order:

1. Leg Press	9. Lat Pulldown
2. Leg Curl	10. Shoulder Shrug
3. Leg Extension	11. Upright Row
4. Heel Raise	12. Bicep Curl
5. Foot Flexion	13. Tricep Extension
6. Bench Press	14. Wrist Curl/Reverse Wrist Curl
7. Rowing	15. Sit-Ups/Leg Raises
8. Seated Press	16. Neck Exercises

Leg Press

Equipment Used: Leg press station
Major Muscles Involved: Gluteus maximus, quadriceps
Description of Exercise:
1. Sit with shoulders against seat back and balls of feet centered on foot pads.
2. Adjust seat so that knee joints are less than a 90° angle.
3. Loosely grip handles.
4. Straighten both legs but do not "lock out" as the thigh muscles will be allowed to relax.
5. Pause, slowly recover to starting position and repeat.

Important Points:
1. Do not grip handles tightly.
2. Do not bounce weight stack at bottom of movement.

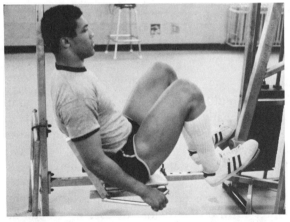

Leg Press: Starting Position

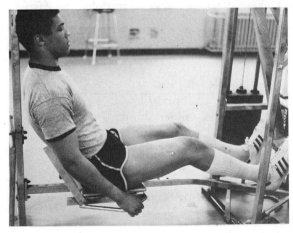

Leg Press: Pause Position

Leg Curl

Equipment Used: Leg curl station
Major Muscles Involved: Hamstrings
Description of Exercise:
1. Lay face down on bench.
2. Place back of ankles under roller pads with kneecaps just off end of bench.
3. Curl legs upward as far as possible.
4. Pause, slowly recover to starting position and repeat.
Important Points:
1. Feet should be in a flexed position with toes pointing towards knees.
2. Feet should be at least perpendicular in the contracted position.

Leg Curl: Starting Position

Leg Curl: Pause Position

Leg Extension

Equipment Used: Leg extension station
Major Muscles Involved: Quadriceps
Description of Exercise:
1. In a seated position, place both feet behind roller pads with back of knees against front of seat.
2. Keep head and shoulders in a vertical position throughout exercise.
3. Raise feet until both legs are straight.
4. Pause, slowly recover to starting position and repeat.

Important Points:
1. Grip side of bench loosely with hands.
2. Relax hands, neck, and face muscles during exercise.

Leg Extension: Starting Position

Leg Extension: Pause Position

Heel Raise

Equipment Used: Seated press station
Major Muscles Involved: Calves
Description of Exercise:
1. Stand facing weight stack.
2. Grip handles with overhand grip and raise weights to shoulder level.
3. Place balls of feet on block of wood.
4. Elevate heels as high as possible.
5. Pause, slowly recover to starting position and repeat.

Important Points:
1. Do not let heels touch ground.
2. Do not bend knees.

Heel Raise: Starting Position   *Heel Raise: Pause Position*

Foot Flexion

Equipment Used: Leg curl station
Major Muscles Involved: Tibialis anterior
Description of Exercise:
1. In a seated position place three cushions under calves.
2. Place toes under roller pads.
3. Keep torso in a vertical position and loosely grip sides of bench.
4. Curl toes back towards knees as far as possible.
5. Pause, slowly recover to starting position and repeat.
Important Points:
1. Allow feet to extend completely on negative movement.
2. Cushions may be added or subtracted for comfort.

Foot Flexion: Starting Position

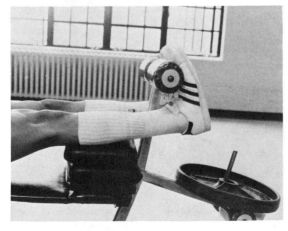

Foot Flexion: Pause Position

Bench Press

Equipment Used: Bench press station
Major Muscles Involved: Pectorals, deltoids, triceps
Description of Exercise:
1. Lay flat on bench with knees bent and feet flat on floor.
2. Adjust bench so handles are aligned with center of chest.
3. Grip handles with an overhand grip slightly wider than shoulder width.
4. Straighten arms until elbows are fully extended.
5. Pause, slowly recover to starting position and repeat.

Important Points:
1. A block of wood may be placed under head of bench for a greater range of movement.
2. Do not arch back.
3. Do not bounce weight stack at bottom.
4. Exhale while raising weight.

Bench Press: Starting Position

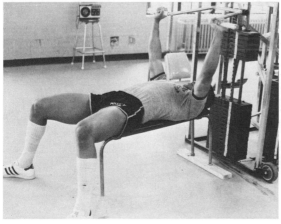

Bench Press: Pause Position

Rowing

Equipment Used: Bicep curl station
Major Muscles Involved: Latissimus dorsi, rhomboids, biceps
Description of Exercise:
1. Sit on floor with legs extended and torso in a vertical position.
2. Grip handles with an overhand grip and hands shoulder width apart.
3. Pull bar as close to center of chest as possible.
4. Pause, slowly recover to starting position and repeat.
Important Points:
1. If weight stack is touching bottom in extended position place a 45 pound plate between base of machine and feet.

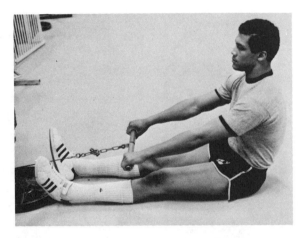

Rowing: Starting Position

Rowing: Pause Position

Seated Press

Equipment Used: Seated press station
Major Muscles Involved: Deltoids, triceps
Description of Exercise:

1. Sit on stool facing away from weight stack.
2. Adjust seat so that handles are directly above shoulders.
3. Grip handles with an overhand grip slightly wider than shoulder width.
4. Place feet on bottom rung of stool.
5. Straighten arms overhead until elbows are completely extended.
6. Pause, slowly recover to starting position and repeat.

Important Points:

1. If a strain is placed on the lower back in the extended position, seat may be too far from weight stack.
2. Do not arch back.

Seated Press: Starting Position

Seated Press: Pause Position

Lat Pulldown

Equipment Used: Lat pulldown station
Major Muscles Involved: Latissimus dorsi, biceps
Description of Exercise:
1. Assume a kneeling position facing weight stack.
2. Grip curved handles on bar.
3. Pull bar downward and touch base of neck.
4. Pause, slowly recover to starting position and repeat.
Important Points:
1. A sitting position may be used if preferred.
2. A closer grip may be used to place more emphasis on the biceps.

Lat Pulldown: Starting Position   *Lat Pulldown: Pause Position*

Shoulder Shrug

Equipment Used: Bench press station
Major Muscles Involved: Trapezius
Description of Exercise:
1. Stand between bench press handles facing weight stack.
2. Grip inside of handles with an overhand grip.
3. Keep arms straight and raise shoulders upward as high as possible.
4. Pause, slowly recover to starting position and repeat.
Important Points:
1. Keep body perfectly straight.
2. Allow arms to drop as far as possible on the negative movement without bending back.

Shoulder Shrug: Starting Position   *Shoulder Shrug: Pause Position*

Upright Row

Equipment Used: Bicep curl station
Major Muscles Involved: Trapezius, deltoids, biceps
Description of Exercise:
1. Stand facing bicep curl station and grip handles with an overhand grip narrower than shoulder width.
2. Pull bar upward until bar touches bottom side of chin.
3. Pause, slowly recover to starting position and repeat.
Important Points:
1. Stand straight with head up throughout the exercise.
2. Keep elbows pointed to outside.
3. Pull bar all the way to chin.

Upright Row: Starting Position   *Upright Row: Pause Position*

Bicep Curl

Equipment Used: Bicep curl station
Muscles Involved: Biceps
Description of Exercise:
1. Stand with arms extended downward facing bicep curl station.
2. Grip bar shoulder width apart using underhand grip.
3. Curl bar forward and upward keeping elbows back until bar touches base of neck.
4. Pause, slowly recover to starting position and repeat.

Important Points:
1. Do not allow elbows to come forward.
2. Do not lean back during exercise.

Bicep Curl: Starting Position   *Bicep Curl: Pause Position*

Tricep Extension

Equipment Used: Lat pulldown station
Muscles Involved: Triceps
Description of Exercise:
1. Stand facing pulldown station with feet shoulder width apart.
2. Grip bar with overhand grip less than shoulder width apart.
3. Pull bar downward until elbows are at sides.
4. Push hands downward until arms are extended.
5. Pause, slowly recover to starting position and repeat.

Important Points:
1. Elbows must be kept at sides.
2. Wrapping thumbs over bar makes it easier to stabilize wrists.
3. For greater range of movement, wrap towel around the cable junction of the bar gripping both sides of the towel and extend towel downward.

Tricep Extension: Starting Position

Tricep Extension: Pause Position

Tricep Extension: Using Towel

68

Wrist Curl

Equipment Used: Bicep curl station
Major Muscles Involved: Forearm flexors
Description of Exercises:
1. Sit on the end of an exercise bench with forearms resting on knees.
2. Grasp handles with an underhand grip and raise until weight stack is lifted.
3. Allow handles to rest on finger tips.
4. Curl bar up toward elbows as far as possible.
5. Pause, slowly recover to starting position and repeat.

Important Points:
1. Keep forearms flat on thighs throughout exercise.
2. Wrists should be just over end of knees.

Wrist Curl: Starting Position

Wrist Curl: Pause Position

Reverse Wrist Curl

Equipment Used: Bicep curl station
Major Muscles Involved: Forearm extensors
Description of Exercise:
1. Sit on the end of an exercise bench with forearms resting on knees.
2. Grasp handles with an overhand grip.
3. Curl bar up toward elbows as far as possible.
4. Pause, slowly recover to starting position and repeat.
Important Points:
1. Keep forearms flat on thighs throughout exercise.
2. Wrists should be just over end of knees.

Reverse Wrist Curl: Starting Position   *Reverse Wrist Curl: Pause Position*

Sit-Ups

Equipment Used: Incline Board
Muscles Involved: Abdominals, hip flexors
Description of Exercise:
1. Lay face up on incline board with knees bent.
2. Hook feet under rollar pads and interlace fingers behind head.
3. Curl torso upward and forward to a point just short of being perpendicular with floor.
4. Pause, slowly recover to starting position and repeat.

Important Points:
1. Keep knees bent.
2. When more than 15 repetitions can be performed raise end of bench one level higher.
3. Lower torso slowly during negative movement.
4. Begin next repetition immediately.

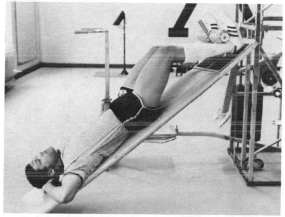

Sit-Up: Starting Position

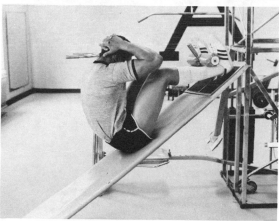

Sit-Up: Pause Position

Leg Raises

Equipment Used: Incline board
Muscles Involved: Abdominals, hip flexors
Description of Exercise:
1. Lay face up on incline board with knees and elbows slightly bent.
2. Grip post at top of board.
3. Raise legs upward and forward until knees are perpendicular with floor.
4. Pause, slowly recover to starting position and repeat.
Important Points:
1. When more than 15 repetitions can be performed move board one level higher.
2. Lower legs slowly during negative movement.

Leg Raises: Starting Position

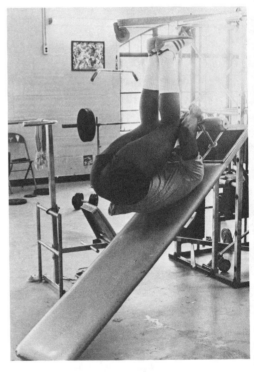

Leg Raises: Pause Position

Sample Universal Workout

Monday and Friday

Exercise	Number of Sets
Leg Press	3
Leg Curl	2
Leg Extension	2
Heel Raise	2
Foot Flexion	2
Bench Press	3
Rowing	3
Seated Press	2
Lat Pulldown	2
Shoulder Shrug	2
Upright Row	2
Bicep Curl	2
Tricep Extension	2
Wrist Curl	1
Reverse Wrist Curl	1
Sit-Ups	1
4 Way Neck with Partner	1

Wednesday

Exercise	Number of Sets
Leg Press	2
Leg Curl	1
Leg Extension	1
Bench Press	2
Rowing	2
Seated Press	1
Lat Pulldown	1
Bicep Curl	2
Tricep Extension	2
Leg Raises	1

Nautilus machines permit an athlete to perform a high intensity workout in approximately 20-30 minutes.

4 NAUTILUS EXERCISES

The ownership of Nautilus equipment is not quite as widespread as either free weight equipment or the Universal Gym. Undoubtedly, this is the case because Nautilus equipment has been on the market only in the last ten years and because it is relatively expensive (comparatively). The major advantages of Nautilus equipment are: the machines provide full range exercise, each machine isolates a specific muscle group, the variable resistance capability of Nautilus allows a muscle to be exhausted in one set, and a high intensity workout can be completed in approximately 20-30 minutes.

The principles stated in Chapter 1 should be followed in addition to these basic techniques:

1. On machines where seat adjustment and body position can be varied, make adjustments so that the center of the axis of the cam is directly aligned with the center of the joint that is being exercised.
2. Do not twist or move body during the exercise.
3. Maintain a loose comfortable grip with hands.
4. Begin with a weight that can be done comfortably for 8 repetitions.
5. For cardiorespiratory conditioning move quickly from one machine to the next.
6. Compound and double machines are designed to use a single joint exercise to pre-exhaust a muscle and then a mulitiple joint exercise to cause a further state of exhaustion on the same muscle. Example: On the compound leg machine perform the leg extension to the point of momentary failure then immediately perform the leg press.

This chapter includes descriptions and pictures of Nautilus exercises, and a sample Nautilus workout. For best results, the order of exercises should be performed as follows:

1. Hip and Back	9. Super Pullover
2. Leg Extension	10. Torso Arm Pulldown
3. Leg Press	11. Double Shoulder
4. Leg Curl	12. Shoulder Shrug
5. Heel Raise	13. Bicep Curl
6. Foot Flexion	14. Tricep Extension
7. Double Chest	15. Wrist Curls/Reverse Wrist Curls
8. Dips/Chins	16. 4-Way Neck

One of the primary advantages of Nautilus equipment is that it provides a full-range of movement during each exercise.

DUO/POLY HIP AND BACK MACHINE

Hip Extension

Major Muscles Involved: Gluteus maximus, spinal erectors
Description of Exercise:
1. Lay on back with legs over roller pads.
2. Align hip joints with center of rotation cams.
3. Fasten seat belt snugly around waist and grasp handles lightly.
4. Extend both legs at same time and push back with hands.
5. Hold one leg in fully extended position and allow other leg to bend up and back as far as possible.
6. Extend bent leg downward until it is even with extended leg.
7. Arch lower back and force both legs downward.
8. Pause, repeat same action with other leg.

Important Points:
1. When legs are fully extended in contracted position, keep knees straight and together and point toes downward.
2. When one leg is bending backward in the negative movement do not allow extended leg to raise upward.

Hip and Back: Starting Position

Hip and Back: Pause Position

COMPOUND LEG MACHINE

Leg Extension

Major Muscles Involved: Quadriceps

Description of Exercise:

1. In a seated position, place both feet behind roller pads with back of knees against front of seat.
2. Adjust seat back so that it touches lower back.
3. Keep head and shoulders against seat back throughout exercise.
4. Raise feet until both legs are straight.
5. Pause, recover to starting position and repeat.

Leg Extension: Pause Position

Leg Extension: Starting Position

Leg Press

Major Muscles Involved: Gluteus maximus, quadriceps
Description of Exercise:
1. Flip down foot pads.
2. Place feet on pads with toes turned slightly inward.
3. Push both legs outward until knees are straight.
4. Pause with knees slightly bent, slowly recover to starting position and repeat.

Important Points:
1. Move immediately from leg extension to leg press.
2. Relax hands, neck, and face muscles during exercise.

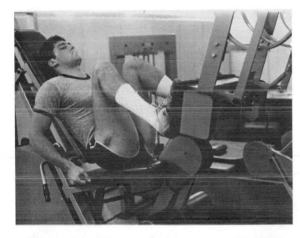

Leg Press: Starting Position

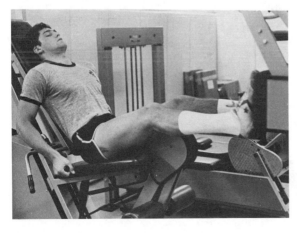

Leg Press: Pause Position

LEG CURL MACHINE

Leg Curl

Major Muscles Involved: Hamstrings
Description of Exercise:
1. Lay face down on machine.
2. Place back of ankles under roller pads with kneecaps just off end of bench.
3. Grip handles loosely.
4. Curl legs upward attempting to touch buttocks with roller pads.
5. Pause, slowly recover to starting position.

Important Points:
1. Feet should be flexed with toes pointing towards knees throughout exercise.
2. Allow hips to rise off of bench when nearing full contraction.

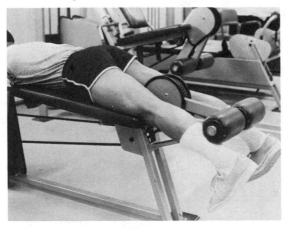

Leg Curl: Starting Position

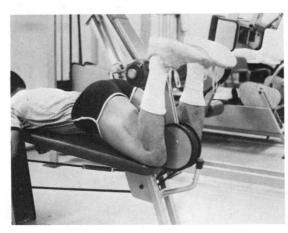

Leg Curl: Pause Position

MULTI-EXERCISE MACHINE

Heel Raise

Major Muscles Involved: Calves
Description of Exercise:
1. Adjust belt comfortably around hips.
2. Place balls of feet on first step with hands on top step and back parallel to floor.
3. Keep knees locked throughout exercise.
4. Raise heels as high as possible.
5. Pause, slowly recover to starting position and repeat.

Important Points:
1. Do not lean forward.
2. Attempt to flex toes upward at bottom of movement to allow for maximum stretch.

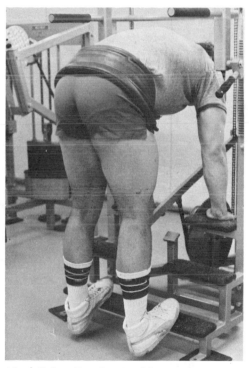

Heel Raise: Starting Position

Heel Raise: Pause Position

LEG CURL MACHINE

Foot Flexion

Major Muscles Involved: Tibialis Anterior

Description of Exercise:

1. In a seated position place three cushions under calves and place toes under roller pads.
2. Keep torso in a vertical position and grip sides of bench loosely.
3. Curl toes up towards knees as far as possible.
4. Pause, slowly recover to starting position and repeat.

Important Points:

1. Allow feet to extend completely on negative part of movement.
2. This exercise should always be performed when the heel raise is performed.

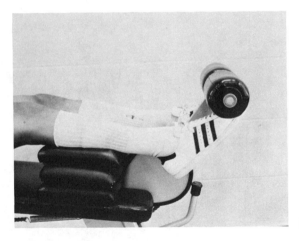

Foot Flexion: Starting Position

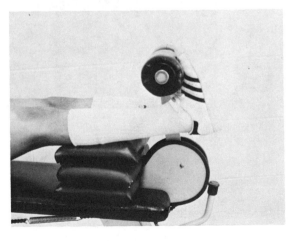

Foot Flexion: Pause Position

DOUBLE CHEST MACHINE

Arm Cross

Major Muscles Involved: Pectoralis major, deltoids

Description of Exercise:

1. Adjust seat until center of shoulders are directly beneath center of overhead cams.
2. Fasten seat belt.
3. Place forearms behind movement arm pads.
4. Grip handles loosely (use whichever handle will place elbow at 90° angle).
5. Keep head and shoulders back and push elbows together until movement arms touch.
6. Pause, slowly recover to starting position and repeat.

Arm Cross: Starting Position

Arm Cross: Pause Position

Decline Press

Major Muscles Involved: Pectorals, deltoids, triceps
Description of Exercise:
1. Use foot pad to bring handles forward.
2. Grip handles with overhand grip and remove feet from pad.
3. Push handles forward until arms are extended.
4. Pause with elbows slightly bent, slowly recover to starting position and repeat.

Important Points:
1. Perform decline press immediately after completing arm cross.
2. Keep head and shoulders against seat back throughout both movements.

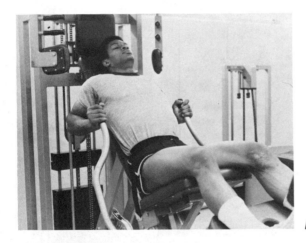

Decline Press: Starting Position

Decline Press: Pause Position

MULTI/EXERCISE MACHINE

Parallel Dip

Major Muscles Involved: Pectorals, deltoids, triceps
Description of Exercise:
1. Adjust carriage high enough so that knees will not hit the steps during the exercise.
2. Climb steps and suspend weight with elbows locked and knees bent.
3. Slowly lower body until elbows are less than 90° (this is the starting position).
4. Extend arms until elbows are straight.
5. Pause, slowly recover to starting position and repeat.

Parallel Dip: Starting Position   *Parallel Dip: Pause Position*

Chins

Major Muscles Involved: Latissimus Dorsi, biceps
Description of Exercise:
1. Place crossbar in forward position and adjust carriage to a point where the chin is just over the bar when standing on top step.
2. Grasp crossbar with an underhand grip and suspend weight with arms straight and knees bent.
3. Pull body upward until chin is over bar.
4. Pause, slowly recover to starting position.

Important Points:
1. Negative only repetitions can be performed in both exercises with or without belt.
2. When performing negative only repetitions begin in the up position and slowly lower body (8-10 seconds) then climb steps and repeat.

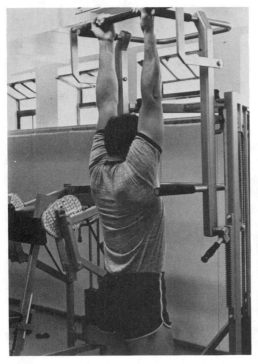

Chins: Starting Position

Chins: Pause Position

SUPER PULLOVER MACHINE

Pullover

Major Muscles Involved: Latissimus dorsi
Description of Exercise:
1. Adjust seat so that center of shoulder joints are aligned with center of cams.
2. Fasten seat belt tightly.
3. Depress foot pedals to move elbow pads forward.
4. Place back of elbows on pads.
5. Hands should be open and leaning against groove in curved portion of bar.
6. Remove feet from foot pedals and allow elbows to move back slowly to a stretched starting position.
7. Rotate elbows forward and downward until crossbar touches hips.
8. Pause, slowly recover to starting position and repeat.

Important Points:
1. Keep head and shoulders against seatback throughout exercise.
2. Keep hands open and relaxed throughout the exercise.
3. Allow elbows to stretch back as far as possible at the completion of each repetition.

Pullover: Starting Position   *Pullover: Pause Position*

TORSO ARM MACHINE

Behind Neck Pulldown

Major Muscles Involved: Latissimus dorsi, biceps
Description of Exercise:
1. Adjust seat low enough so that arms are fully extended when resistance is experienced.
2. Fasten seat belt tightly.
3. Lean forward and grasp handles with palms facing inward.
4. Pull back and downward until base of neck is touched.
5. Pause, slowly recover to starting position and repeat.

Important Points:
1. Be sure that arms are fully extended when negative movement is completed.
2. Keep a forward lean throughout exercise.

Behind Neck Pulldown: Starting Position

Behind Neck Pulldown: Pause Position

DOUBLE SHOULDER MACHINE

Side Lateral Raise

Major Muscles Involved: Deltoids
Description of Exercise:
1. Adjust seat so that center of shoulder joints are aligned with center of cams.
2. Fasten seat belt.
3. Place back of wrists on pads and grip handles loosely.
4. Raise elbows until arms are parallel with floor.
5. Pause, slowly recover to starting position and repeat.

Side Lateral Raise: Starting Position   *Side Lateral Raise: Pause Position*

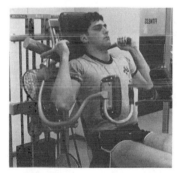

Overhead Press: Starting Position   *Overhead Press: Pause Position*

Overhead Press

Major Muscles Involved: Deltoids, triceps
Description of Exercise:
1. Grasp handles behind shoulders.
2. Straighten arms overhead.
3. Pause, slowly recover to starting position and repeat.
Important Points:
1. Perform overhead press immediately after side lateral raise.
2. Keep legs over end of seat.
3. Do not arch back.

NECK AND SHOULDER MACHINE

Shoulder Shrug

Major Muscles Involved: Trapezius

Description of Exercise:

1. Take a seated position and place forearms between pads.
2. Keep palms open and facing upward.
3. Straighten back so that weight stack is lifted. If weight stack is not lifted in this position, place cushions on seat.
4. Raise shoulders as high as possible.
5. Pause, slowly recover to starting position and repeat.

Important Points:

1. Do not lean back or use legs during exercise.
2. Do not straighten arms.
3. Check for good form and relaxed facial muscles in attached mirror.

Shoulder Shrug: Starting Position

Shoulder Shrug: Pause Position

MULTI CURL MACHINE

Two Arm Curl

Major Muscles Involved: Biceps
Description of Exercise:
1. In a seated position place elbows on pad aligned with center of cams.
2. Adjust seat so that shoulders are lower than elbows.
3. Curl both arms until wrists are just in front of neck.
4. Pause, slowly recover to starting position and repeat.

Two Arm Curl: Pause Position

Two Arm Curl: Starting Position

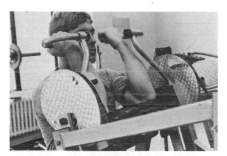

Alternate Curl: Starting Position

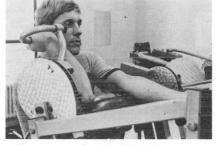

Alternate Curl: Pause Position

Two Arm Alternate Curl

Major Muscles Involved: Biceps
Description of Exercise:
1. Same starting position as two arm curl.
2. Curl both arms up to neck and pause.
3. Do one complete repetition with one arm.
4. Do the next repetition with the other arm.
5. Continue alternate repetitions until both arms reach momentary failure.
Important Points:
1. Allow arms to extend completely on negative movement.
2. Keep head and torso in a vertical position.

MULTI TRICEPS MACHINE

Tricep Extension

Major Muscles Involved: Triceps
Description of Exercise:
1. In a seated position place elbows on pad aligned with center of cams.
2. Adjust seat so that shoulders are lower than elbows.
3. Extend both arms until elbows are straight.
4. Pause, slowly recover to starting position.

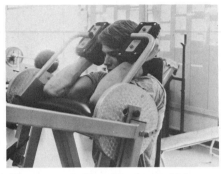

Tricep Extension: Starting Position

Tricep Extension: Pause Position

Alternate Tricep Extension: Starting Position

Alternate Tricep Extension: Pause Position

Alternate Tricep Extension

Major Muscles Involved: Triceps
Description of Exercise:
1. Same starting position as tricep extension.
2. Extend both arms until straight and pause.
3. Do one complete repetition with one arm.
4. Do the next repetition with the other arm.
5. Continue alternate repetitions until both arms reach momentary failure.

Important Points:
1. Keep back and head in a vertical position.
2. Insure that arms reach and hold full extension in pause position.

MULTI EXERCISE MACHINE

Wrist Curl

Major Muscles Involved: Forearm flexors
Description of Exercise:
1. Sit on the end of an exercise bench with forearms resting on knees.
2. Grasp handles with an underhand grip and raise until weight stack is lifted.
3. Allow handles to rest on finger tips.
4. Curl bar up towards elbows as far as possible.
5. Pause, slowly recover to starting position and repeat.

Wrist Curl: Starting Position

Wrist Curl: Pause Position

Reverse Wrist Curl: Starting Position

Reverse Wrist Curl: Pause Position

Reverse Wrist Curl

Major Muscles Involved: Forearm extensors
Description of Exercise:
1. Same starting position as wrist curl only grip bar with an overhand grip.
2. Curl bar up towards elbows as far as possible.
3. Pause, slowly recover to starting position and repeat.
Important Points:
1. Keep forearms flat on thighs throughout exercise.
2. Wrists should be just over end of knees.

4-WAY NECK MACHINE

Anterior Flexion

Major Muscles Involved: Anterior flexors

Description of Exercise:

1. Face machine and adjust seat so that nose is in center of pads.
2. Grip handles and keep torso in a vertical position.
3. Push head towards chest.
4. Pause, slowly recover to starting position and repeat.

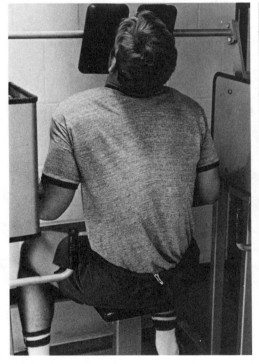 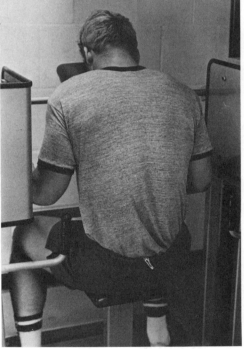

Anterior Flexion: Starting Position   *Anterior Flexion: Pause Position*

Posterior Extension

Major Muscles Involved: Posterior extensors
Description of Exercise:
1. Adjust seat so that base of neck is aligned with center of cam.
2. Grip handles and keep torso in a vertical position.
3. Extend head as far back as possible.
4. Pause, slowly recover to starting position and repeat.

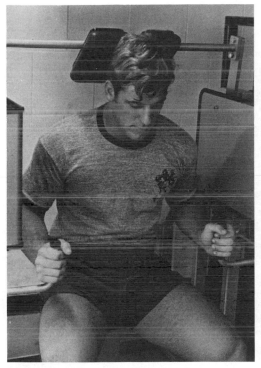 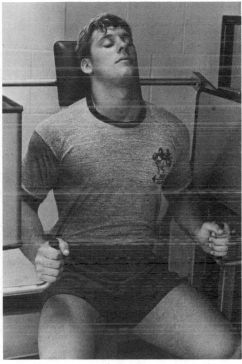

Posterior Extension: Starting Position   *Posterior Extension: Pause Position*

Lateral Flexion-Left and Right

Major Muscles Involved: Lateral flexors
Description of Exercise:
1. Adjust seat so that right rear is in center of pads.
2. Grip handles and keep torso in a vertical position.
3. Move head towards right shoulder.
4. Pause, slowly recover to starting position and repeat.
5. Upon completion perform the same exercise with the left side.

Important Points:
1. Always move head in a smooth manner.
2. Always perform neck exercises last.

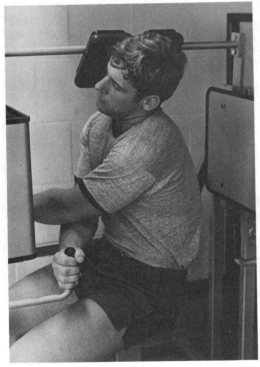
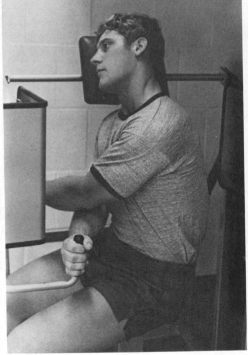

Lateral Flexion: Starting Position   *Lateral Flexion: Pause Position*

Sample Nautilus Workout

Monday
Partner assisted
negative workout

1. Hip and Back
2. Leg Extension
3. Leg Press
   (Partner assisted negatives)
4. Leg Curl
   (Partner assisted negatives)
5. Heel Raise
6. Foot flexion
7. Arm Cross
8. Decline Press
   (Partner assisted negatives)
9. Dips (Negative only)
10. Super pullover
    (Partner assisted negatives)
11. Torso Arm Pulldown
    (Partner assisted negatives)
12. Chins (Negative only)
13. Side Lateral Raise
14. Overhead Press
    (Partner assisted negatives)
15. Shrugs
16. Bicep Curl
    (Partner assisted negatives)
17. Tricep Extension
    (Partner assisted negatives)
18. Wrist Curls
19. 4-Way Neck

Wednesday—No negatives

1. Hip and Back
2. Leg Extension
3. Leg Press

4. Leg Curl
5. Arm Cross
6. Decline Press
7. Super Pullover
8. Torso Arm Pulldown
9. Side Lateral Raise
10. Overhead Press
11. Shrug
12. Bicep Curl (alternate)
13. Tricep Extension (alternate)

Friday—Negative accentuated
workout

1. Hip and Back
2. Leg Extension
   (Negative accentuated)
3. Leg Press
4. Leg Curl
   (Negative accentuated)
5. Heel Raise
6. Foot Flexion
7. Arm Cross
8. Decline Press
   (Negative accentuated)
9. Dips
10. Super Pullover
11. Chins
12. Side Lateral Raise
13. Overhead Press
    (Negative accentuated)
14. Shrugs
15. Bicep Curl
16. Tricep Extension
17. Wrist Curls
18. 4-Way Neck

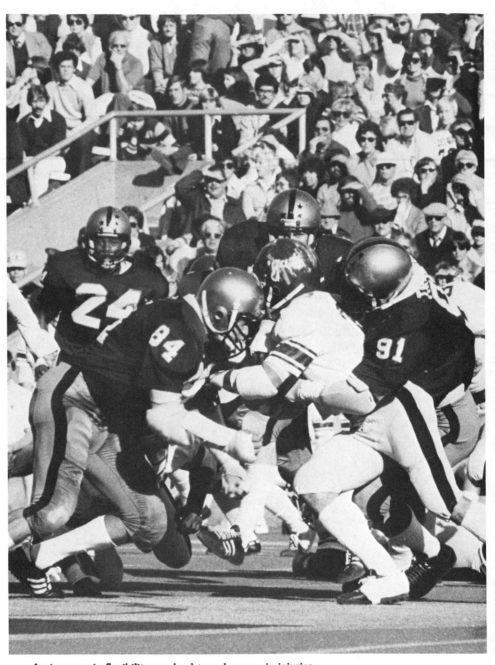

An increase in flexibility can lead to a *decrease* in injuries.

5 BLACK KNIGHT'S FLEXIBILITY PROGRAM

Flexibility is defined as the maximal range of movement for a joint. The degrees of flexibility are effected by the surrounding connective tissue. This includes ligaments (attaches bone together), tendons (attaches muscle to bone), and muscles (causes movement of the joint). Ligaments are slightly extensible but do not have a great deal of elasticity. Muscle tissue on the other hand does have elasticity and therefore stretching this tissue permits more efficient joint movement. Elasticity refers to the amount of stretch the tissue can incur when force is applied and then return to its resting length. Extensibility is the amount the tissue can stretch without resulting in damage. For muscle tissue this amount is approximately 50%. In Chapter 1, several methods of increasing flexibility through strength training were discussed but it should be noted that the continual practice of stretching particularly prior to rigorous athletic performance will not only improve performance but help to reduce the chances of injury.

This chapter presents the flexibility program of the West Point football team and also explains the proper method of stretching.

The stretching program should always be supervised by the coaching staff if it is to be done properly. Each practice session should begin with 15 minutes of stretching, since this session not only will help flexibility but also provide a good warm-up. In order to maintain flexibility, stretching exercises must be included in the year around conditioning program. It is extremely important that the stretching program be well organized since time wasted on the field results in less time for skill improvement. In order to achieve maximal results, the following principles must be strictly adhered to:
1. Perform each movement in a slow, deliberate manner. Any bouncing or jerking may lead to injury.

2. Perform every exercise correctly. Performing the exercise incorrectly only compromises the results.
3. Start with a slow easy stretch and continue the stretch to the point of a burning sensation, hold in that position, then recover.
4. Repeat the same exercise attempting to stretch a little further.
5. Begin each stretching session with a light jog to increase the circulation of the blood to the muscles.

FLEXIBILITY EXERCISES

Bend and Reach

Area Stretched: Lower back, Hamstrings
Description of Exercise:
1. Stand with legs straight and feet shoulder width apart.
2. Torso vertical with hands on hips.
3. Slowly bend forward at the waist and reach for the ground behind the feet.
4. Hold for 8 counts, recover to starting position and repeat.
Important Points:
1. Bend slowly and do not bounce.
2. Attempt to touch ground behind feet.
3. Attempt to stretch further on second repetition.
4. Do not allow knees to bend.

Bend and Reach

Toe Touch

Area Stretched: Lower back, hamstrings, calves
Description of Exercise:
1 Stand with legs straight and feet together.
2. Torso vertical with hands on hips.
3. Slowly bend forward at the waist and touch hands to the ground.
4. Hold for 8 counts, recover to starting position and repeat.
Important Points:
1. Bend slowly.
2. Keep legs straight.
3. Do not bounce.

Toe Touch

Lateral Hip and Groin Stretch

Lateral Hip and Groin Stretch

Area Stretched: Hips, hamstrings
Description of Exercise:
1. Stand with left leg extended to left side, toe pointing forward and inside of foot touching ground.
2. Right foot pointing to right, right knee bent and right hand on right thigh.
3. Torso vertical.
4. Bend right knee with torso upright until maximum stretch occurs on left hip.
5. Hold for 8 counts, recover to starting position and repeat.
6. After the stretch is completed on one leg do the same exercise with opposite leg.
Important Points:
1. Keep extended leg straight.
2. Extend leg far enough to the side to allow maximum stretch.
3. Do not bounce.
4. Keep torso vertical.

Achilles and Calve Stretch

Area Stretched: Calves and achilles tendon

Description of Exercise:

1. Bend left knee and extend right leg as far back as possible with ball of foot on ground.
2. Keeping right leg straight slowly lower right heel down towards ground.
3. Hold for 8 counts, recover to starting position and repeat.
4. When completed do same exercise with opposite leg.

Important Points:

1. Keep right leg straight.
2. If heel touches ground extend leg further back.
3. Lower slowly as the achilles tendon can be easily injured with a jerky motion.

Achilles and Calve Stretch

Wall Stretch for Calves

Wall Stretch for Calves

Area Stretched: Calves, achilles tendon

Description of Exercise:

1. Place palms on wall and lean against wall at least at a 45° angle.
2. Extend both legs as far back as possible keeping balls of feet on ground.
3. Slowly lower heels down towards ground.
4. Hold for 8 counts, recover to starting position and repeat.

Important Points:

1. Keep both legs straight.
2. If heels touch ground extend legs further back.
3. Lower heels slowly.

Hurdlers Hamstring Stretch

Area Stretched: Hamstrings
Description of Exercise:
1. Assume seated hurdlers position with right leg extended, left knee bent, left toes pointed straight back and torso vertical.
2. Slowly bend forward at waist.
3. Touch nose to knee while reaching with both hands for heel of extended foot.
4. Hold for 8 counts, recover to starting position and repeat.
5. When exercise is completed perform same exercise with opposite leg.
Important Points:
1. Keep extended leg straight.
2. Bend forward slowly and recover fully between repetitions.

Hurdlers Hamstring Stretch   *Hurdlers Quad Stretch*

Hurdlers Quad Stretch

Area Stretched: Quadriceps, hips
Description of Exercise:
1. Assume seated hurdlers position with right leg extended, left knee bent, left toes pointed straight back and torso vertical.
2. Slowly lean torso backwards as far as possible.
3. Hold for 8 counts, recover to starting position and repeat.
4. When exercise is completed perform same exercise with opposite leg.
Important Points:
1. Keep bent knee in contact with ground.
2. Use hands for support when leaning backwards and recovering to starting position.

Hip Rotator Stretch

Area Stretched: Lower back, buttocks, hips
Description of Exercise:
1. Lay on back with arms extended to sides at shoulder level.
2. Extend both legs.
3. Bend right knee and rotate knee across left side of body.
4. Grasp right knee with left hand and pull knee downward and up toward left shoulder until maximum stretch is felt.
5. Hold for 8 counts, recover to starting position and repeat.
6. When exercise is completed perform same exercise with opposite leg.
Important Points:
1. Keep right shoulder flat on ground throughout exercise.
2. Keep left leg extended.

Hip Rotator Stretch

Seated Hamstring Stretch

Seated Hamstring Stretch

Area Stretched: Lower back, hamstrings
Description of Exercise:
1. Sit with both legs extended slightly wider than shoulder width apart.
2. Bend forward at waist attempting to touch nose to ground and at same time reach both hands to feet.
3. Hold for 8 counts, recover to starting position and repeat.
Important Points:
1. Avoid fast, bouncing movement.
2. Keep legs straight.

Seated Hamstring and Calve Stretch

Area Stretched: Lower back, hamstrings, calves
Description of Exercise:
1. Sit with both legs extended and heels together.
2. Bend forward at waist attempting to touch nose to ground and at same time reach both hands to feet.
3. Hold for 8 counts, recover to starting position and repeat.

Important Points:
1. Avoid fast, bouncing movement.
2. Keep legs straight.
3. Keep feet flexed for greater calve stretch.

Seated Hamstring and Calve Stretch

Partner Groin Stretch

Partner Groin Stretch

Area Stretched: Groin
Description of Exercise:
1. Sit with knees bent, soles of feet touching each other, and heels pulled in toward groin.
2. Partner kneels in front with hands on inside of partner's knees.
3. Partner slowly pushes knees down until maximum stretch is experienced.
4. Hold for 8 counts, recover to starting position and repeat.

Important Points:
1. Partner should apply slow, steady pressure.
2. Partners must communicate so that the proper amount of pressure is applied.

Partner Chest Stretch

Area Stretched: Shoulders, pectorals
Description of Exercise:
1. Sit on ground with legs extended, hands interlaced behind head and elbows back.
2. Partner stands behind with side of one leg supporting partners back and hands on inside of partner's elbows.
3. Partner stretches elbows back to point of maximum stretch with a slow deliberate movement.
4. Hold for 8 counts, recover to starting position and repeat.

Important Points
1. Partners must communicate so that the correct point of tension is reached.
2. Bring elbows completely forward between repetitions.

Partner Chest Stretch

Partner Shoulder Stretch

Partner Shoulder Stretch

Area Stretched: Shoulders, pectorals
Description of Exercise:
1. Sit on ground with legs extended, hands interlaced behind head and elbows back.
2. Partner stands behind with side of one leg supporting partners back and hands on inside of partner's elbows.
3. Partner stretches elbows back and then upward to point of maximum stretch with a slow deliberate movement.
4. Hold for 8 counts, recover to starting position and repeat.

Important Points:
1. Partners must communicate so that the correct point of tension is reached.
2. Bring elbows completely forward between repetitions.

Partner Neck Stretch—Anterior Flexion

Area Stretched: Anterior flexors
Description of Exercise:
1. Assume a kneeling position on all fours and raise head.
2. Partner places hands on front of forehead.
3. While partner applies resistance, slowly move head down to chest, pause, slowly recover to starting position keeping with 8 count.

Anterior Flexion

Posterior Extension

Lateral Flexion: Left

Lateral Flexion: Right

Partner Neck Stretch—Posterior Extension

Area Stretched: Posterior extensors
Description of Exercise:
1. On all fours with chin tucked to chest.
2. Partner places hands on back of head.
3. While partner applies resistance, slowly move head up and back as far as possible, pause, slowly recover to starting position keeping with 8 count.

Partner Neck Stretch—Lateral Flexion

Area Stretched: Lateral flexors
Description of Exercise:
1. On all fours with head rotated to right.
2. Partner places hands and knee (for added support) on left side of head.
3. While partner applies resistance move head across to left shoulder, pause, slowly recover to starting position keeping with 8 count.
4. When left side is completed repeat exercise with right side.
Important Points:
1. Movement must be slow and smooth in all directions.

Standing-Partner Hamstring Stretch

Area Stretched: Hamstrings
Description of Exercise:
1. Standing on right leg, raise left leg forward to waist level, toes pointing upward and heel resting in partner's hands.
2. Bend forward at waist and attempt to touch nose to knee.
3. Hold for 8 counts, recover to starting position and repeat.
4. When exercise is completed perform same exercise with opposite leg.
Important Points:
1. Keep both legs straight throughout entire exercise.
2. Extended leg should be held at waist level or higher.

Standing Partner Hamstring Stretch   *Standing-Partner Groin Stretch*

Standing-Partner Groin Stretch

Area Stretched: Hamstrings, groin
Description of Exercise:
1. Standing on right leg, raise left leg forward to waist level, toes pointing to the right and foot resting in partner's hands.
2. Bend slowly over right side and attempt to touch palms to ground in front of right foot.
3. Hold for 8 counts, recover to starting position and repeat.
4. When exercise is completed perform same exercise with opposite leg.
Important Points:
1. Keep both legs straight throughout entire exercise.
2. Extended leg should be held at waist level.

6 TOTAL "YEAR AROUND" CONDITIONING

The strength and conditioning program for successful football teams is rapidly becoming a year around program. Many of the advantages of a strength program have already been stated. It is a well documented fact that every explosive movement made by a football player in practice or during a game is primarily the result of muscular strength. Stronger muscles enable the player to hit harder, run faster, kick further, and block and tackle successfully. It is also a key ingredient in injury prevention and rehabilitation.

A factor that has not been discussed yet in any detail is muscular endurance. It is endurance that enables a football player to minimize fatigue which frequently limits athletic performance. Developing a high state of endurance for a football player is certainly not as comprehensive as increasing muscular size and strength but there are numerous advantages for including endurance training in the year around program. These advantages include: Increased efficiency of the heart and lungs, maintenance of body fat, and general toning of the running muscles and other connective tissue. In order to receive these benefits and achieve a training effect, it is necessary to reach a certain level of stress. If done properly, conditioning can occur rather quickly. It should also be noted that fitness vanishes quickly when it is neglected. In order to gain and maintain an adequate level of fitness, the conditioning should occur at least every other day with no long layoffs during the year.

The methods used by the football staff at Army for conditioning are aerobic and anaerobic running, agility drills, and high intensity strength workouts. Sample year around programs are presented at the end of the chapter.

Running Program

Many football players simply don't know how to run properly. Because of this lack of knowledge, we place a great deal of emphasis on form running. The first step in improving running ability is to increase flexibility. Simply by increasing the flexibility of the hip and knee joint, an athlete may be able to improve his stride by two or three inches. In a twenty yard dash, this increase in stride would amount to almost two feet. This two feet can mean the difference of breaking a tackle, making a tackle, or completing a first down. Specific methods of improving flexibility were discussed in detail in Chapter 5.

In addition to improving flexibility, a great deal of time is spent on form running. This includes basic running mechanics: Head alignment, body angle, alignment of hips and knees, and foot placement.

Form Running Drills

The first thing to work on in form running is the arm swing. Keeping the elbow at a 90° angle allows the arm to swing quickly and powerfully. Since the movement of the arms directs leg movement, this short arm swing results in short, fast movements of the legs. It is essential that the arms swing straight ahead as this keeps the center of gravity moving in the desired path. The elbows should pass close to the hips and the backward swing should bring the arm to a point where if dropping the hand straight down it would land in the rear pocket. On the forward swing, the hand should not reach higher than shoulder level.

The next area of concentration is on foot movement. The first phase begins by running in place, lifting each foot six inches off the ground, and landing on the ball of the foot only. After running in place for 10 seconds, the athlete begins moving down the field concentrating on the following skills:

a. Vigorous arm swing
b. Bouncing off ball of foot only.
c. Keeping arms from going across body.
d. Good body lean.
e. Running with hips and knees pointed straight ahead.

The next drill is a "quick step" drill which is done in the same manner, only the athlete concentrates on pumping the arms and legs as fast as possible for 30 yards with very little forward lean. The athlete should still concentrate on technique and not on how fast he can run the 30 yards.

Once the quick step drill has been practiced, the athletes move into "high stepping". This is similar to the "quick step" drill only the knees are lifted to chest level. Each stride should only cover two or three feet maximum. This is practiced for a distance of 20 yards.

Items On Which To Concentrate On Form Running

1. Run on toes and ball of foot.
2. Drive off of back foot.
3. Keep hands relaxed.
4. Swing arms straight forward and back.
5. Maintain a good body lean.
6. Run in a straight line.
7. Keep heels off of ground.
8. Drive knees upward and forward.
9. Maintain a good balance.
10. Run relaxed.

After practicing form running drills on short distance repetitions, the same form running should be practiced over 100 yard distances. As mentioned in Chapter 7, periodic 20 yard and 40 yard sprints are administered to evaluate success.

Aerobic and Anaerobic Training

When energy is produced in the absence of an adequate supply of oxygen, the anaerobic system is functioning. This would result from an intense workout up to approximately 15 seconds in duration. Football is a perfect example of an anaerobic activity. Since a play seldom exceeds 15 seconds in length, there is definitely a critical need for anaerobic fitness. The body must be capable of rapidly replenishing muscle glycogen stores for the next play. Anaerobic fitness is developed through short intense workouts.

The word aerobic means "with or in the presence of oxygen." Where a sufficient supply of oxygen is available to the muscles, a continual supply of energy is produced. This generally occurs in activities of greater than 3 minutes in duration such as the one mile run. An overlap of the aerobic and anaerobic system occurs between 15 seconds and three minutes depending on the intensity of the workout. Even though football is an anaerobic activity, the aerobic system pays back the energy depletions between plays in a game. For this reason aerobic fitness also becomes a must. Developing this type of fitness requires the athlete to raise the heart rate to 75% of maximum and hold it there for at least 15 minutes. Different types of running will effect both systems. The types of running activities are listed below:

Acceleration Sprinting: This involves a gradual increase in speed from a jog to a sprint e.g. jog for 25 yards, run ½ to ¾ speed for 25 yards, then sprint for 50 yards.

Repetition Running: Running distances of ½ to ¾ mile allowing complete recovery (walking) between each run.

Fast Interval Running: Intensity of work interval is at least ¾ speed. Athlete jogs during relief intervals (period between work intervals where partial recovery of heart rate occurs).

Slow Interval: The work interval is roughly ½ to ¾ speed. The relief intervals are jogged and are three times as long as the work interval.

Jog Sprints: Sprints followed by equal distance of jogging in between.

Interval Sprints: Short sprints of 50-60 yards followed by short jogs of 20-30 yards and repeated for 2 or more miles.

Repetition Sprints: Maximum speed over short distances allowing a near complete recovery.

Long Slow Distance: Running a long distance at a slow pace.

Agility Drills

While agility drills are no substitute for practicing the skill itself, they do assist in conditioning the athlete and preparing him to practice the skills. Many of these drills provide the athlete with help in developing coordination, balance, speed, and quickness of the feet. These agility drills include *jumping rope, forward-backward-sideward rolls, crabwalk, lateral running,* and *backward running.*

High Intensity Strength Training

The exercises in most strength workouts are performed in short bursts of 30-45 seconds followed by a brief recovery period. Training in this method is very effective for building strength but does nothing for cardiovascular endurance. The traditional methods of endurance training are accomplished by running a certain distance that will raise the heart rate to three quarters of maximum for 15 minutes. Certain types of weight workouts can accomplish endurance training at the same time as strength training. The heart does not know which muscles are being worked to raise the heart rate. Exercising the arms can have the same effect on the heart and lungs as exercising the legs if the amount of work is relatively the same. The method of performing such a strength workout is to perform each exercise and allow little or no rest to occur between each exercise. If done properly, the heart rate should reach approximately 150 beats per minute by the third or fourth exercise and should remain there for the rest of the workout. Endurance is being increased by keeping the heart rate at ¾ of maximum for 15-20 minutes.

This method of working out is performed most efficiently on Nautilus equipment. The reason for this is that the point of momentary failure can be reached in only one set.

Although agility drills are not as effective substitutes for skill development as practicing the skill itself, they can help condition the athlete and help develop coordination, balance, speed, and foot quickness.

Off-Season Strength and Conditioning Program

1st WEEK

Monday

Strength Workout—(Free Weights)
Parallel Squat
Dead Lift
Leg Curl
Leg Extension
Bench Press
Parallel Dips—(1 set positive, 1 set negative)
Chins—(1 set positive, 1 set negative)
Bent over Row
Seated Press
Shrugs
Bicep Curl
Tricep Extension
Sit-Ups
4-Way Neck

Tuesday

Running and Agility
10 minutes of Flexibility
Jumping Rope
Foot Quickness Drills
Throwing and Catching Medicine Ball
Form Running
Jog ¼ mile
3-40 yd. dashes
Run ½ mile at ¾ speed

Wednesday

Strength Workout—(Nautilus)
Hip and Back
Leg Press
Leg Extension
Leg Curl
Heel Raise
Foot Flexion
Arm Cross
Decline Press
Pullover Torso
Torso Arm
Side Lateral Raise
Seated Press
Shrugs
Bicep Curl
Tricep Extension
Sit-Ups
4-Way Neck

Thursday

Running and Agility
10 minutes of Flexibility
Jumping Rope
Foot Quickness
Lateral Running
Medicine Ball
3-20 yd. sprints
2 mile run at 8 min. pace

Friday

Strength Workout—(Free Weights and Universal)
Parallel Squat—(Barbell)
Dead Lift—(Barbell)
Leg Curl—(Universal)
Leg Extension—(Universal)
Bench Press—(Barbell)
Dips—(Universal)
Lat Pulldowns—(Universal)
Seated Press—(Dumbbells)
Shrugs—(Barbell)
Bicep Curls—(Universal)
Tricep Extensions—(Universal)
Wrist Flexion—(Universal)
Wrist Extension—(Universal)
Leg Raises—(Universal)

2ND WEEK

Monday

Running and Agility
10 minutes of Flexibility
Jog ¼ mile
Run 5-100 yd. sprints with 15 sec. rest between each
Run 3 miles at 8 minute pace

Tuesday

Strength Workout—(Free Weights)
Parallel Squat—(work to maximum 1 rep.)
Dead Lift—(work to maximum 1 rep.)
Leg Curl
Leg Extension
Heel Raise
Foot Flexion
Bench Press—(work to maximum 1 rep.)
Dips—(positive only)
Chins—(positive only)
Seated Press
Shrugs
Bicep Curl
Tricep Extension
Wrist Curl
Wrist Extension
4-Way Neck

Wednesday

Running and Agility
10 minutes of Flexibility
Jumping Rope
Foot Quickness Drills
Medicine Ball
Form Running
5-20 yd. dashes with 15 sec. rest between each
Jog 1 mile

Thursday

Strength Workout—(Free Weights and Nautilus)
Parallel Squat—(Barbell)
Hip and Back—(Nautilus)
Leg Extension—(Nautilus)
Leg Curl—(Nautilus)
Bench Press—(Barbell)
Arm Cross—(Nautilus)
Pullover—(Nautilus)
Torso Arm—(Nautilus)
Seated Press—(Nautilus)
Shrugs—(Nautilus)
Bicep Curl—(Dumbbells)
Tricep Extension—(Barbell)
Sit-Ups
4-Way Neck—(Nautilus)

Friday

Running and Agility
Jog ¼ mile
15 minutes of Flexibility
3-40 yd. dashes for time
3-20 yd. dashes for time
2 mile run at 8 min. pace

In-Season Conditioning Program

EVERY WEEK

Sunday

Strength Workout—(Free weights & Nautilus)
Parallel Squat—(Barbell)
Dead Lift—(Barbell)
Leg Curl—(Nautilus)
Leg Extension—(Nautilus)
Heel Raise—(Nautilus)
Foot Flexion—(Nautilus)
Bench Press—(Barbell)
Dips
Chins
Pullover—(Nautilus)
Seated Press—(Nautilus)
Shrugs—(Nautilus)
Bicep Curl—(Nautilus)
Tricep Extension—(Nautilus)
Sit-Ups
4-Way Neck—(Nautilus)

Monday

Football Practice
¼ mile jog
12 minutes of Flexibility
20 minutes of Agility
Practice
8-100 yd. sprints with 15 sec. rest
   between each

Tuesday

Football Practice
¼ mile jog
12 minutes of Flexibility
20 minutes of Agility
Practice

5-100 yd. sprints with 30 sec. rest
   between each
¼ mile jog

Wednesday

Football Practice
¼ mile jog
12 minutes of Flexibility
Practice
30 min. strength workout—(Nautilus)
Hip & Back
Leg Extension
Leg Press
Arm Cross
Decline Press
Pullover
Chins
Seated Press
Bicep Curl
Tricep Ext.
4-Way Neck

Thursday

Football Practice
¼ mile jog
12 minutes of Flexibility
20 minutes of Agility
Practice
4-100 yd. sprints
¼ mile jog

Friday

REST

Saturday

GAME

7 EVALUATION AND MOTIVATION

A football player must engage in a properly designed strength training program on a year-around basis in order to maintain the size and strength necessary to perform well on the playing field. During the season the major objective of a strength training program should be to maintain the level of strength that has been developed in the off-season. During the off-season the major objective should be to motivate the athletes and to drive them to develop greater strength gains. Along with motivation, a successful developmental fitness program should involve specific methods of evaluating the effects of the program. Since many of the evaluative methods practiced at West Point serve as motivators, they will be discussed concurrently.

Body Weight

The maintenance of an ideal body weight is an extremely important factor to the football athlete. It should be noted that the key factor is "ideal" body weight rather than "maximum" body weight. With the exception of organs and bodily fluids, body weight is a composite of muscle, bones, and fat. Body fat has almost no function to a football player. The only possible benefit from excess fat is to provide a cushion to the body, however, nearly all of the necessary cushion is provided by the uniform pads. Therefore, excess body fat contributes nothing to performance and means that an athlete carrying 20 extra pounds of body fat would compete on equal terms with an individual who carried a 20 pound pack on his back.

Figure 7-1.

It is muscle tissue that permits movement of the body and subsequent power. The objective of optimal performance for a football player should be to gain as much muscle as possible and reduce body fat to a minimum. The method used at West Point for determining the amount of body fat is accomplished by using skinfold calipers (Fig 7-1). By measuring the thickness of subcutaneous fat at various sites on the body, an individual's body fat percentage can be calculated (Figures 7-2 to 7-5). A lineman weighing 250 pounds with 20% body fat is carrying 50 pounds of fat while the same lineman at 250 pounds with 10% body fat is only carrying 25 pounds of fat and will be much quicker. The ideal percentage of body fat varies for each individual. A working goal for Army football is to have all linemen less than 15% body fat and all backs less than 12%.

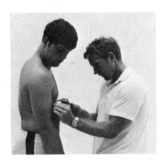

Figure 7-2.

Figure 7-3.

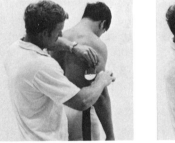

Figure 7-4.

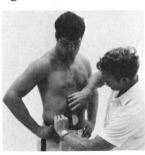

Figure 7-5.

Figure 7-6.

Testing Speed

Measurements of the speed of an athlete are taken periodically by administering the 20 yard dash and the 40 yard dash. Both measures are taken on all players. While being tested on each of the dashes, the athletes start from a sprinters stance (Fig 7-6). The distance is measured for accuracy. Three coaches are involved in timing each athlete. One coach is the starter and two coaches are on the finish line with stop watches. The coaches on the finish line average the difference between their watches for the finish time. Each athlete takes three attempts at each distance, with complete recovery between each attempt. The fastest of the three times is recorded for each dash.

Testing Cardiovascular Endurance

As a test of cardiovascular endurance, each athlete is given a two mile run test just before the fall two-a-day practices begin. The goal for this test is to have each athlete run the two miles in less than 15 minutes.

Testing Power

Power is tested by measuring vertical jump ability. Markers are placed on a wall at one inch intervals from approximately 72 inches to 144 inches. The athlete stands with the side of one foot against the wall, stretching one arm as high as possible, with both heels in contact with the floor. After the measurement is recorded in inches, the athlete dips his fingers in chalk dust

119

and jumps vertically (starting with same foot against wall), touching his fingers as high as possible on the marker with the same hand used in the initial measure (Figures 7-7, 7-8). The vertical jump is the difference between the starting measure and the finishing mark. For example, an athlete's first measure is 80 inches and the chalk dust touches a point on the marker at 102 inches. The vertical jump is 22 inches. Each athlete is given three attempts.

Figure 7-7.   **Figure 7-8.**

Testing Strength

Measuring an athlete's strength is accomplished in three areas. The "dead lift" measures the strength level of the lower back and upper legs; the "squat" measures the strength level of the buttocks and upper legs; and the "bench press" measures the strength level of the chest, shoulders, and arms. The methods for performing these lifts were discussed in Chapter 2.

Additional Motivators

Of all the fitness aspects evaluated, the easiest factor to change is muscular strength. Each of the aspects can be improved by strength training. Since the greatest gains occur in the "lift" measurements, we provide additional motivators. These motivators include: Awarding of shirts indicating amount lifted, a wall chart displaying the amount of weight lifted by each athlete on the three lifts, and occasional power lifting meets.

Figure 7-9.

300-400 lb. Bench Press Shirts

The ability to lift a large amount of weight in the bench press for one maximum repetition does not accurately predict the ability of an athlete to play football. It does, however, give him a basis of comparison and a certain amount of confidence in knowing that he is as strong or stronger than his opponent in that lift. As an incentive to lift more weight, shirts with a monogram indication of the amount lifted in 25 pound increments are awarded to athletes successfully lifting that amount (Fig 7-9).

Pride Board

The "pride board" contains much of the testing information. The greatest amount of competition between the athletes occurs in the "bench press", "dead lift", "squat", and "total" columns. Each athlete's name is placed on the board in each column. Next to the names of the athletes are two figures: The top figure indicates the amount lifted and the bottom figure is the percentage of that amount in body weight. Ranking on the board is done by percentage of body weight. For example: Lifter "A" weighs 200 lbs. and deadlifts 450 lbs., Lifter "B" weighs 250 lbs. and dead lifts 500 lbs. Lifter "A" has lifted 225% of his body weight and would receive a higher ranking than lifter "B" who lifted 200% of his body weight. This gives an incentive for all athletes as they are competing by relative body weight.

Lifting Meets

All athletes are invited to participate in a power lifting meet in the spring at West Point. The meet is open to any student at the Academy. Medals are awarded to the top three finishers in each weight class. The objective is to total as much poundage as possible in the squat, bench press, and dead lift. Competition in the meet is intensive. By having AAU officials conduct the event, the athletes are encouraged to practice the lifts in the correct manner.

There is no evidence whatsoever to indicate that athletic performance can be improved by modifying a well balanced diet.

8 NUTRITION AND DRUGS

In recent years athletes have developed a keen interest in nutrition and other ergogenic aids which purport to affect athletic performance. Unfortunately, some athletes are too easily influenced by the success of other athletes whose diet may have included supplements thought to include "miraculous" components for improving athletic performance. In most cases the success of such an athlete was achieved in spite of—not because of—the dietary supplements. At the present time, there is no evidence *whatsoever* to indicate that athletic performance can be improved by modifying a well balanced diet. It should be noted, however, that less-than-a-basically-sound diet can cause athletic performance to go downhill. The belief that a football player must consume tremendous amounts of meat and other protein supplements is simply unfounded. The purpose of this chapter is to present information on some of the more "visible" nutritional constituents and drugs that are thought to effect athletic performance.

PROTEIN AND CARBOHYDRATES

Protein

Proteins are the building blocks of muscle tissue. Nearly 15% of the human body is composed of protein. Muscle tissue alone is made up of approximately 22% protein. It is the amino acids in protein that rebuild and maintain muscle tissue when it is broken down. Because of this, a common misconception exists where athletes believe that the more protein they ingest the larger their muscle tissue will become. It is a well-documented fact that the body is only capable of assimilating a certain amount of protein. The remainder is simply excreted by the body. Numerous studies have indicated that the total requirement for protein in a 24 hour period for growth and muscle hypertrophy is approximately .8 grams per 1 kilogram of body weight. A normal balanced diet provides more than that amount of protein. Further indications are that excessive amounts of protein over a prolonged period of time can result in damage to the liver.

Foods that contain protein are meats, fish, eggs, cheese, poultry, milk and other milk products. Protein supplements can be quite expensive and provide no benefit above a normal balanced diet.

Typical foods high in protein.   *Typical foods high in carbohydrates.*

Carbohydrates

Carbohydrates are broken down into glucose (simple sugar) when digested and are used as an immediate energy supply. Unlike protein, excessive carbohydrates are not immediately excreted but stored in the body in the form of body fat. A combination of a high carbohydrate diet and low activity generally results in an overweight individual. Sources of carbohydrates are breads, pastries, candies, fruits, cereal, potatoes, soft drinks, and starches.

Regardless of the activity it is important not to overindulge in carbohydrate loaded foods as it does not result in increased energy but rather increased body fat.

VITAMINS

Vitamin A valuable in helping the body resist infections; functions in promoting healthy eye tissues and eye adaption in dim light.
Vitamin A Sources: Liver, green and yellow vegetables, dairy products.

Vitamin C aids in preventing and counteracting infection; hastens the healing of wounds and bones; aids in preventing fatigue in athletes; helps prevent muscle soreness in body builders.
Vitamin C Sources: Citrus fruits, tomatoes, melons, cabbage.

Vitamin D essential in helping the body utilize calcium and phosphorus which are necessary for proper skeletal growth.
Vitamin D Sources: Cod-liver oil, tuna fish, egg yolks, sunlight.

Vitamin E prevents cell destruction and breakdown of body tissues; serves as a vasodilator which allows more blood to flow through the circulatory system.
Vitamin E Sources: Wheat germ, whole grains, meat, eggs, liver, leafy vegetables.

Vitamin K aids in the proper clotting of blood; helps the liver function correctly.
Vitamin K Sources: Liver, eggs, leafy green vegetables, cauliflower.

MINERALS

Niacin aids in utilization of energy; promotes healthy skin, nerves and digestive tract, aids digestion and fosters normal appetite.
Niacin Sources: Liver, meat, poultry, fish, peanuts, fortified cereal products.

Calcium provides structure and strength to bones and teeth; assists in clotting blood; functions in normal muscle contraction and relaxation.
Calcium Sources: Milk, yogurt, cheese, sardines, salmon, mustard, turnip greens.

Iron aids in utilization of energy; prevents nutritional anemia and fatigue; increases resistance to infection; combines with protein to form hemoglobin, the red substance in blood that carries oxygen to and carbon dioxide from the cells.
Iron Sources: Prune juice, liver, dried beans and peas, red meat.

DRUGS AND WEIGHT TRAINING

Tobacco

It has long been believed that smoking greatly reduced the cardiovascular endurance capacity of an athlete. Unfortunately, while common sense leads us to accept the tenet that tobacco is bad for an athlete, only a few studies have examined the relationship between tobacco and physical performance. Many of the problems from tobacco result from the nicotine found in cigarettes. The absorption of nicotine can increase the heart rate by as much as 20 beats per minute and may stay that way for as long as a half hour. Inhaling cigarette smoke also reduces blood flow to the skin and elevates blood pressure which increases the workload of the heart during rest and during exercise.

Alcohol

When alcohol is consumed it immediately goes to the brain and impairs judgement, slows reaction time, and distorts vision. Drinking just prior to athletic performance or weight training can be extremely dangerous since it will impair all of the voluntary muscles. While small amounts of alcohol do not greatly effect strength and endurance, heavy drinking can cause a nutritional deficiency since it destroys many valuable vitamins and minerals in the system. Additionally, a heavy drinking session is usually followed by headaches, nausea, and other unhealthy conditions.

Steroids

The use of Anabolic steroids is one of the foremost drug topics in the athletic world today. The drug very closely resembles the male hormone "testosterone". It is this hormone that brings on the male secondary sex characteristics such as facial hair, deeper voice, and a rapid increase in adolescent growth. The initial intent of the drug was to treat medically disabled patients who had been seriously burned or ill in bed for a long period of time. Misinformed athletes believe that "if a little testosterone is good for muscle growth then a lot must be great". Therefore, they begin taking large doses believing that this will allow them to develop large muscles.

Many experts contend that there is no evidence to substantiate the belief that steroids stimulate muscle growth in healthy, well conditioned athletes. Most research studies on individuals who have used anabolic steroids have concluded that there were no significant advantages in groups that took steroids as opposed to groups who trained without use of the drug.

Anyone taking steroids must be aware of the potentially dangerous side effects. Steroids affect the liver, the kidneys, and the endocrine system. Side effects from continued use may include: Voice changes, increased amounts

There is no evidence *to support the belief that the use of steroids stimulates muscle growth in healthy, well conditioned athletes.*

of bodily hair, headaches, loss of sex drive, and even insomnia. Anabolic steroids hold a much higher risk for teenagers than for adults. Since it is during this stage where the secondary sex characteristics occur, it is also during this stage when the greatest danger exists. In extreme cases it can even cause premature slowing down of bone growth and result in a shorter body structure.